W9-DBO-188

English: Intermediate Literature A
Student Guide

Second Edition

Part 2

Illustrations Credits

All illustrations © K12 Inc. unless otherwise noted

About K12 Inc.

K12 Inc., a technology-based education company, is the nation's leading provider of proprietary curriculum and online education programs to students in grades K–12. K¹² provides its curriculum and academic services to online schools, traditional classrooms, blended school programs, and directly to families. K12 Inc. also operates the K¹² International Academy, an accredited, diploma-granting online private school serving students worldwide. K¹²'s mission is to provide any child the curriculum and tools to maximize success in life, regardless of geographic, financial, or demographic circumstances. K12 Inc. is accredited by CITA. More information can be found at www.K12.com.

ISBN 978-1-60153-424-8

Printed by Courier, Kendallville, IN, USA, April 2014

Table of Contents

Classics

Unit 10: A Matter of Justice

Unit 11: Stories of Our Time

Unit 12: To Everything There Is a Season

Unit 13: You need to select a novel for this unit.

Unit 14: Stuff and Nonsense

Unit 15: *Twelfth Night*

Unit 16: Stories from the Bible

Unit 17: You need to select a novel for this unit.

Unit 18: Semester Review and Assessment Novels List

Student Guide
Lesson 1: "The Wisdom of Solomon"

You are going to be surprised when you hear how this judge plans to solve a dispute between two women.

Lesson Objectives

- Describe characters by speech, actions, or interactions with others.
- Identify character traits and motivations.
- Make inferences and draw conclusions.
- Contribute meaningfully to group discussions by being prepared for discussion, drawing on preparation, explaining own ideas, building upon others' comments, and asking questions.

PREPARE

Approximate lesson time is 60 minutes.

Materials

For the Student

MLA Handbook for Writers of Research Papers - MLA (Modern Language Association) Full citation: MLA Handbook for Writers of Research Papers. 7th ed. New York: MLA, 2009. Print.

Classics for Young Readers, Vol. 6 - pages 194-195

Reading Notebook

Optional

⌨ Guidelines for Peer Discussion

LEARN
Activity 1: "The Wisdom of Solomon" (Offline)

Activity 2: "The Wisdom of Solomon" (Online)

Activity 3: Solomon's Wise Judgment (Online)

Activity 4: Writing Your Own Proverb (Offline)

Instructions

Read these proverbs from around the world:

Examine what is said, not him who speaks.
Do not protect yourself by a fence, but rather by your friends.
If you see no reason for giving thanks, the fault lies in yourself.
Adversity brings knowledge and knowledge, wisdom.
A friend in need is a friend indeed.
As you sow, so shall you reap.
Better die with honor than live in shame.
Experience is the mother of wisdom.

In the past, proverbs were used to help people remember a valuable truth. Because proverbs were short, people could memorize them and pass them on to their children.

Now you are going to write your own proverb based on today's story.

First, consider what truths Solomon may have revealed in his method with the two women:

- Does Solomon say that some people are worthy of justice and not others, or does he show that all people deserve justice?

- Which does he show is more effective: harsh judgment or gentle prodding?

- Is he a wise and caring ruler or an uninterested and harsh one?

Then, focus on the truth you want to state in your proverb. Maybe you want to focus on the way Solomon judges the case, or maybe you want to focus on the behavior of the women. Maybe you even want to focus on the baby! Think about the story's situation from as many different angles as you can. Write down any ideas that the story conveys to you about life. Then revise your statement so that it is brief and powerful. Many proverbs use concrete images or figurative language in which some specific object, action, or creature stands for a general truth. "As you sow, so shall you reap" is one such proverb. If it were only about sowing and reaping, no one would remember it except farmers! But in fact, its underlying truth applies to all kinds of situations.

When you have phrased your proverb as vividly as you can, record it in your Reading Notebook and check for spelling and grammar errors.

Activity 5. Optional: "The Wisdom of Solomon" (Online)

Activity 6: Peer Discussion (Offline)

Guidelines for Peer Discussion

Share your thoughts, ideas, questions, and feelings about a text with a peer or others. Listen carefully to what everyone has to say about the text. During your discussion, follow these guidelines.

1. Be prepared to discuss your ideas about the text and to ask and answer questions about what you read. Whenever possible, use examples from the text to support your statements, help others understand your meaning, and justify your answers.

2. Listen carefully and quietly if it's not your turn to speak. Pay attention to what others say so that you can add your ideas. Speak clearly and in complete sentences.

3. Connect and add to the ideas that others have stated using sentences that begin with phrases such as:

   "I understand . . . ."
   "I feel that . . . ."
   "We should also think about how . . . ."
   "That idea relates to . . . ."

4. Respectfully question the opinions of others and politely defend your reasoning if your opinion differs. Use sentences that begin with phrases such as:

   "What do you mean when you say . . .?"
   "Can you give an example of . . .?"
   "I see what you're saying, but what about . . .?"
   "I reacted to that a little differently because . . . ."
   "I disagree with that because . . . ."

5. Draw conclusions about what has already happened in a text and make inferences about what may happen next.

6. Keep the goal(s) of the discussion in mind and respect others. Remember that each member of the group has a valuable contribution to make.

7. Remember that opinions are neither right nor wrong, only different. Remain cordial, thoughtful, and courteous when disagreements or differences of opinion occur.

Student Guide
Lesson 2: "A Just Judge"

Solomon must have had a creative mind to think up the scheme for judging the women in the previous lesson. Today you will meet another clever judge.

Lesson Objectives
- Form opinions and personal responses after reading.
- Make inferences and draw conclusions.
- Describe characters by speech, actions, or interactions with others.
- Identify character traits and motivations.

PREPARE

Approximate lesson time is 60 minutes.

Materials
For the Student

Classics for Young Readers, Vol. 6 - pages 196-200

LEARN
Activity 1: "A Just Judge" *(Online)*

Activity 2: "A Just Judge" *(Offline)*

Activity 3: "A Just Judge" *(Online)*

Activity 4: Deductive Reasoning *(Online)*

Activity 5: Paying for Justice *(Offline)*
Instructions
Answer the questions about the concept of justice.

1. The famous philosopher Socrates is credited with the proverb, "Justice is its own reward." What does this mean? Do you think the judge in today's story believed that? Why or why not?

   _____

   _____

   _____

   _____

   _____

   _____

2. Do you think the wise judge in the story suspects that receiving payment from the king would not be wise? Why might taking money be a bad idea for a judge?

   _____

   _____

   _____

   _____

   _____

   _____

Student Guide
Lesson 3: "Ooka and the Honest Thief"

If your family were starving, would you break the law to steal food for them? Sometimes right and wrong are not easy to distinguish, as you will see in this story.

Lesson Objectives

- Identify irony.
- Make inferences and draw conclusions.
- Describe characters by speech, actions, or interactions with others.
- Identify character traits and motivations.

PREPARE

Approximate lesson time is 60 minutes.

Materials

For the Student

Classics for Young Readers, Vol. 6 - pages 201-206

Keywords and Pronunciation

irony : the effect of language in which the intended meaning is the opposite of what is stated; or the effect of a situation in which the opposite of what one would have thought is actually what occurs

oxymoron (ahk-see-MOR-ahn) : a phrase that includes two contradictory parts, such as jumbo shrimp

LEARN
Activity 1: "Ooka and the Honest Thief" *(Online)*

Activity 2: "Ooka and the Honest Thief" *(Offline)*

Activity 3: "Ooka and the Honest Thief" *(Online)*

Activity 4: Gonta and Ooka *(Online)*

Activity 5: Think About It *(Offline)*

Instructions

Answer the questions about this story.

1. How do you think Gonta feels when he reads the note at the end of the story?

   _____

   _____

   _____

   _____

   _____

2. Who is the wisest man in the story?

   _____

   _____

   _____

   _____

   _____

3. Are you surprised by the outcome of the story? Why or why not?

   _____

   _____

   _____

   _____

   _____

4. What would you have done if you were Gonta?

   _____

   _____

   _____

   _____

   _____

Student Guide
Lesson 4: Reflection

Perhaps you have already noticed similarities among the judges in the first three stories. In this lesson, you will explore their similarities and differences.

Lesson Objectives
- Compare and contrast literary characters and selections.
- Identify character traits and motivations.

PREPARE

Approximate lesson time is 60 minutes.

LEARN
Activity 1: Compare and Contrast the Judges *(Online)*

Activity 2: Codebreaker *(Online)*

Activity 3: Considering Justice *(Offline)*
Instructions
Now spend some time reflecting on the way justice is carried out in the three stories that you have read. Answer the questions.

1. What is justice? Write your own definition.

   _____

   _____

   _____

   _____

2. Do you think each of the three judges is just? Why or why not?

   _____

   _____

   _____

   _____

   _____

---

3. What is the difference between justice and mercy? Explain, and give at least one example of each quality from the stories.

    _____

    _____

    _____

    _____

4. Does the culture in which the story takes place affect the handling of justice? How? Can you give an example from our own country?

    _____

    _____

    _____

    _____

    _____

5. How important is it for a society to have a method for carrying out justice? Explain your answer.

    _____

    _____

    _____

    _____

    _____

Student Guide
Lesson 5: "The Convict and the Bishop": Session 1

In this lesson, you will meet <u>Jean Valjean</u>, a French peasant who has just been released from 19 years in prison. As you read, remember your own ideas about justice as they have developed through your reading of the previous three stories. Who is being just and unjust in this story?

Lesson Objectives
- Make inferences and draw conclusions.
- Describe characters by speech, actions, or interactions with others.
- Identify character traits and motivations.
- Identify irony.

PREPARE

Approximate lesson time is 60 minutes.

Materials
> For the Student
> > Classics for Young Readers, Vol. 6 - pages 207-218

Keywords and Pronunciation

irony : the effect of language in which the intended meaning is the opposite of what is stated; or the effect of a situation in which the opposite of what one would have thought is actually what occurs

Jean Valjean (zhahn val-ZHAHN)

Les Miserables (lay mihz-ur-AH-bluh)

protagonist (proh-TAG-uh-nist) : the main character; the character around whom the action of the plot centers

---

LEARN
Activity 1: "The Convict and the Bishop" - Session 1 *(Online)*

Activity 2: "The Convict and the Bishop" - Session 1 *(Offline)*

Activity 3: "The Convict and the Bishop" - Session 1 *(Online)*

Activity 4: Characterization *(Online)*

Activity 5: Jean Valjean *(Offline)*

Instructions

1. We know from the story's introduction why Valjean first goes to prison and why he stays so long. Does this information make any difference to you, the reader?

   _____

   _____

   _____

   _____

   _____

2. Does Valjean receive justice in his first crime? Compare his treatment with the treatment of Gonta by Ooka.

   _____

   _____

   _____

   _____

   _____

3. What do you think Valjean's intentions are when he goes to the very first inn?

   _____

   _____

   _____

   _____

   _____

4. The townspeople are immediately suspicious of Valjean, and their treatment of him gets worse and worse. Is their prejudice against him fair? Why or why not? What does their behavior suggest?

   _____

   _____

   _____

   _____

Activity 6. Optional: "The Convict and the Bishop" - Session 1 *(Online)*

Student Guide
Lesson 6: "The Convict and the Bishop": Session 2

Will Valjean find a place to stay? Why does the woman point him to the door by the bishop's palace? Read on to find out.

Lesson Objectives

- Describe characters by speech, actions, or interactions with others.
- Identify character traits and motivations.
- Make inferences and draw conclusions.

PREPARE

Approximate lesson time is 60 minutes.

Materials

For the Student

Classics for Young Readers, Vol. 6 - pages 219-226

Keywords and Pronunciation

irony : the effect of language in which the intended meaning is the opposite of what is stated; or the effect of a situation in which the opposite of what one would have thought is actually what occurs

Jean Valjean (zhahn val-ZHAHN)

Les Miserables (lay mihz-ur-AH-bluh)

Monseigneur (mahn-sayn-YUHR)

LEARN
Activity 1: "The Convict and the Bishop" - Session 2 *(Offline)*

Activity 2: "The Convict and the Bishop" - Session 2 *(Online)*

Activity 3: Differing Perceptions *(Online)*

Activity 4: The Words of the Priest *(Online)*

Activity 5: The Bishop's Way *(Offline)*

Instructions

1. Early in their conversation the bishop reaches out and touches Valjean's hand. Why do you think this might be a significant gesture?

   _____

   _____

   _____

   _____

   _____

2. At end of Part 2, Valjean turns to the bishop in a harsh voice and says,
   "'Ah, now, indeed! You lodge me in your house, as near you as that?' He checked himself, and added with a laugh in which there was something horrible, 'Have you reflected upon it? Who tells you I am not a murderer?' The bishop responded, 'God will take care of that.'"
   Why do you think Valjean says what he does? Does the bishop fear Valjean? Why or why not?

   _____

   _____

   _____

   _____

   _____

3. Think about the way the bishop judges Valjean compared to the way the other townspeople do. Is the safe judgment always the best judgment?

   _____

   _____

   _____

   _____

   _____

Student Guide
Lesson 7: "The Convict and the Bishop": Session 3

Jean Valjean has met a kind and generous man. Will he be able to move beyond the pain of his past and make a new life for himself?

Lesson Objectives

- Describe characters by speech, actions, or interactions with others.
- Identify character traits and motivations.
- Identify irony.

PREPARE

Approximate lesson time is 60 minutes.

Materials

For the Student

Classics for Young Readers, Vol. 6 - pages 226-233

Keywords and Pronunciation

conflict : a clash or struggle between people, ideas, or feelings; characters can have a conflict within themselves, with another character, with society, or with nature

irony : the effect of language in which the intended meaning is the opposite of what is stated; or the effect of a situation in which the opposite of what one would have thought is actually what occurs

Jean Valjean (zhahn val-ZHAHN)

Les Miserables (lay mihz-ur-AH-bluh)

Monseigneur (mahn-sayn-YUHR)

LEARN
Activity 1: "The Convict and the Bishop" - Session 3 *(Online)*

Activity 2: "The Convict and the Bishop" - Session 3 *(Offline)*

Activity 3: "The Convict and the Bishop" - Session 3 *(Online)*

Activity 4: Inner Conflict *(Online)*

Activity 5: Think About It (Offline)
Instructions

1. In Part 2, the bishop says to Valjean: "If you are leaving that sorrowful place with hate and anger against men, you are worthy of compassion; if you leave with good will, gentleness, and peace, you are better than any of us."

    Why is a person full of hatred and anger worthy of compassion?

    _____

    _____

    _____

    Which category does Valjean fall into?

    _____

    _____

    _____

    What about the bishop--doesn't he fall in the second category? Why does he say "better than any of us"?

    _____

    _____

    _____

2. The bishop says at the end of the story: "Forget not--never forget--that you have promised me to use this silver to become an honest man....Jean Valjean, my brother, you belong no longer to evil, but to good. It is your soul that I am buying for you. I withdraw it from dark thoughts and from the spirit of perdition, and I give it to God."

    What is the bishop trying to do?

    _____

    _____

    _____

    How does the bishop "buy" Valjean's soul for him?

    _____

    _____

    _____

3. At the beginning of the story, Valjean "shook his fist at the church." Why does he do that and why is it ironic in the end?

_____

_____

_____

4. What does the bishop know about human nature? What does he hope to accomplish by letting the convict go?

_____

_____

_____

Student Guide
Lesson 8: "Mohandas Gandhi: Truth in Action"

So far in this unit, you have read proverbs and fictional stories about justice and injustice. In this lesson, you will meet a man who fought injustice and mistreatment of an entire nation--the people of India.

Lesson Objectives
- Compare and contrast literary characters and selections.
- Demonstrate knowledge of authors, characters, and events of historically or culturally significant works.
- Describe characters by speech, actions, or interactions with others.
- Identify character traits and motivations.
- Recognize devices used by an author to achieve the purpose, including language, organization, or structure.

PREPARE

Approximate lesson time is 60 minutes.

Materials
For the Student

Classics for Young Readers, Vol. 6 - pages 234-239

LEARN
Activity 1: "Mohandas Gandhi - Truth in Action" *(Offline)*

Activity 2: "Mohandas Gandhi - Truth in Action" *(Online)*

Activity 3: Gandhi's Sense of Justice *(Online)*

Activity 4: Think About It *(Offline)*
Instructions

1. Gandhi was neither a poor man nor an Untouchable. He was a lawyer, educated in England, and well traveled. How do you think his own experiences helped him to fight for justice in India?

_____

_____

_____

_____

2. Compare Gandhi's basis for justice to the ideas of justice expressed in "The Wisdom of Solomon" and "A Just Judge." How are they similar and how are they different?

_____

_____

_____

_____

3. Think about the convict and the bishop from the excerpt from *Les Miserables*. What kind of method does the bishop use to deal with the convict? Compare it to Gandhi's method.

_____

_____

_____

_____

4. Why do you think Gandhi was motivated to practice nonviolence rather than violence? Wouldn't violence have been quicker?

_____

_____

_____

_____

5. Gandhi said, "Nonviolence is the greatest force at the disposal of mankind. It is mightier than the mightiest weapon of destruction devised by the ingenuity of man." How is nonviolence a powerful force? What do you think about nonviolence? Explain your answer.

_____

_____

_____

_____

_____

_____

Activity 5. Optional: "Mohandas Gandhi - Truth in Action" *(Online)*

Student Guide
Lesson 9: "'Equal Justice Under Law': Thurgood Marshall"

Mohandas Gandhi organized the people of India to fight nonviolently the injustice they faced. Today you will meet another man who nonviolently fought injustice toward his own people--African Americans. This man fought injustice by working within the law to change it.

Lesson Objectives
- Describe characters by speech, actions, or interactions with others.
- Identify character traits and motivations.
- Make inferences and draw conclusions.

PREPARE

Approximate lesson time is 60 minutes.

Materials
For the Student

Classics for Young Readers, Vol. 6 - pages 240-246

LEARN
Activity 1: "'Equal Justice Under Law' - Thurgood Marshall" *(Online)*

Activity 2: "'Equal Justice Under Law' - Thurgood Marshall" *(Offline)*

Activity 3: "'Equal Justice Under Law' - Thurgood Marshall" *(Online)*

Activity 4: Marshall's Features *(Online)*

Activity 5: Marshall's Thinking *(Offline)*
Instructions
Answer the following questions about Thurgood Marshall:

1. Why did Marshall face opposition in the African-American community?

   _____
   _____
   _____

---

2. Explain why Marshall did not believe society could be "separate but equal."

_____

_____

_____

_____

_____

3. The author notes that, "A fellow Supreme Court justice said of Marshall, 'No American did more to lead our country out of the wilderness of segregation.'" Look up the word *wilderness* in the dictionary. Why is segregation described as a wilderness? Could you say that all injustice is a "wilderness"? Explain your answer.

_____

_____

_____

_____

_____

_____

_____

_____

_____

_____

Activity 6. Optional: "'Equal Justice Under Law' - Thurgood Marshall" *(Online)*

Student Guide
Lesson 10: Reflection

You have read many stories about justice, but have you had a chance to think about how the concepts of justice that you have explored are similar and different? In today's lesson, you will consider all the stories and prepare for your Unit Assessment.

Lesson Objectives

- Compare and contrast literary characters and selections.
- Describe characters by speech, actions, or interactions with others.
- Identify character traits and motivations.

PREPARE

Approximate lesson time is 60 minutes.

Materials

For the Student

Reading Notebook

LEARN
Activity 1: Fiction vs. Nonfiction *(Online)*

Activity 2: Two Crusaders *(Offline)*
Instructions
A: Two Crusaders

Take a look at the authors' descriptions of the behavior of Gandhi and then Marshall:

"Gandhi went around India by train, meeting and talking with the people. He traveled in crowded third-class compartments with hard benches, and sometimes had to sleep standing up."

"Marshall worked tirelessly on the case, hardly stopping to eat or sleep."

Based on these descriptions of Marshall and Gandhi, can you make a statement that is true about both of them? Respond in your Reading Notebook. Here are some words that you might want to use in your statement:

commitment

dedication

justice

sacrifice

B: Write About It

Consider the following questions about justice and the individuals in this unit. Respond in your Reading Notebook.

Gandhi said, "You must be the change you wish to see in this world."

1. What does this statement mean?

2. How was it true for Gandhi and Marshall?

3. Does it apply to any other characters from stories in the unit? Explain.

Student Guide
Lesson 11: Unit Assessment

Lesson Objectives

- Compare and contrast literary characters and selections.
- Describe characters based on speech, actions, or interactions with others.
- Identify character traits and motivations.
- Identify irony.
- Make inferences and draw conclusions.
- Describe characters by speech, actions, or interactions with others.
- Form opinions and personal responses after reading.
- Identify theme.
- Make inferences and draw conclusions.

PREPARE

Approximate lesson time is 60 minutes.

ASSESS

Unit Checkpoint: "A Matter of Justice," Part 1 (*Online*)

It's time to check what you have learned. Go to the next screen to test your skills.

Unit Checkpoint: "A Matter of Justice," Part 2 (*Offline*)

It's time to check what you have learned.

1. Gather the Assessment Sheet.
2. Read and follow the instructions to complete the assessment.
3. When you've finished, your Learning Coach will review your work and enter the results online.

Student Guide
Lesson 1: "Thank You, M'am": Session 1

Lesson Objectives

- Recognize author's purpose and devices used to accomplish it, including author's language, organization, and structure.
- Formulate opinions and personal responses after reading.
- Describe characters based on speech, actions, or interactions with others.
- Identify character traits and motivations.
- Identify climax.
- Identify conflict and resolution.
- Identify elements of a short story.
- Recognize use of dialect.
- Recognize use of language to convey mood.
- Contribute meaningfully to group discussions by being prepared for discussion, drawing on preparation, explaining own ideas, building upon others' comments, and asking questions.

PREPARE

Approximate lesson time is 60 minutes.

Materials

For the Student

MLA Handbook for Writers of Research Papers - MLA (Modern Language Association) Full citation: MLA Handbook for Writers of Research Papers. 7th ed. New York: MLA, 2009. Print.

Classics for Young Readers, Vol. 6 - pages 262-267

Optional

   📖 Guidelines for Peer Discussion

Keywords and Pronunciation

climax : the point of highest action in a story; the turning point

complicating incident : an important early event that signals that the action is about to start

conflict : a clash or struggle between people, ideas, or feelings; characters can have a conflict within themselves, with another character, with society, or with nature

dialect : a way of speaking that is particular to a certain group of people, place, or time

dialogue : a conversation between characters

exposition : the beginning of a story where the setting, characters, and basic situations are usually introduced

falling action : the part of the plot where issues are resolved and questions are answered

first-person point of view : narration of a story by one of the characters, using the first-person pronouns *I* and *me*

idiom : a phrase or saying particular to a certain place, time, or group of people that is not meant to be understood literally; for example, "to drive one up a wall"

---

mood : the emotions or feelings conveyed in a literary work

resolution : the solution or working out of a literary conflict

rising action : a series of events that builds interest or suspense

setting : where and when a literary work takes place

suspense : excitement and uncertainty about what will happen

theme : the main message that an author wants to communicate to a reader

third-person point of view : narration of a story by an objective outside observer of the action, using the third-person pronouns

LEARN
Activity 1: "Thank You, M'am" - Session 1 *(Online)*

Activity 2: "Thank You, M'am" - Session 1 *(Offline)*

Activity 3: "Thank You, M'am" - Session 1 *(Online)*

Activity 4: "Thank You, M'am" - Session 1 *(Online)*

Activity 5: "Thank You, M'am" - Session 1 *(Online)*

Activity 6: "Thank You, M'am" - Session 1 *(Online)*

Activity 7: Peer Discussion *(Offline)*

Guidelines for Peer Discussion

Share your thoughts, ideas, questions, and feelings about a text with a peer or others. Listen carefully to what everyone has to say about the text. During your discussion, follow these guidelines.

1. Be prepared to discuss your ideas about the text and to ask and answer questions about what you read. Whenever possible, use examples from the text to support your statements, help others understand your meaning, and justify your answers.

2. Listen carefully and quietly if it's not your turn to speak. Pay attention to what others say so that you can add your ideas. Speak clearly and in complete sentences.

3. Connect and add to the ideas that others have stated using sentences that begin with phrases such as:

    "I understand . . . ."
    "I feel that . . . ."
    "We should also think about how . . . ."
    "That idea relates to . . . ."

4. Respectfully question the opinions of others and politely defend your reasoning if your opinion differs. Use sentences that begin with phrases such as:

    "What do you mean when you say . . .?"
    "Can you give an example of . . .?"
    "I see what you're saying, but what about . . .?"
    "I reacted to that a little differently because . . . ."
    "I disagree with that because . . . ."

5. Draw conclusions about what has already happened in a text and make inferences about what may happen next.

6. Keep the goal(s) of the discussion in mind and respect others. Remember that each member of the group has a valuable contribution to make.

7. Remember that opinions are neither right nor wrong, only different. Remain cordial, thoughtful, and courteous when disagreements or differences of opinion occur.

Student Guide
Lesson 2: "Thank You, M'am": Session 2

Now that you have finished reading "Thank You, M'am" and learning about the elements of a short story, spend today exploring the story's themes and symbolism.

Lesson Objectives
- Describe characters based on speech, actions, or interactions with others.
- Identify character traits and motivations.
- Identify symbolism.
- Identify theme.
- Recognize use of language to convey mood.

PREPARE

Approximate lesson time is 60 minutes.

Materials
> For the Student
>> Reading Notebook

Keywords and Pronunciation
dialect : a way of speaking that is particular to a certain group of people, place, or time

symbol : something that stands for something else in literature; for example, a dove may be a symbol for peace

symbolism : the literary technique of using something to stand for or represent another idea; for example, a dove frequently symbolizes peace, while a single red rose sometimes symbolizes love

theme : the main message that an author wants to communicate to a reader

LEARN
Activity 1: "Thank You, M'am" - Session 2 *(Online)*

Activity 2: Strength and Weakness *(Online)*

Activity 3: Blue Suede Shoes *(Online)*

Activity 4: Lessons Learned *(Offline)*

Instructions

1. What does Roger learn over the course of this story?

   _____

   _____

   _____

   _____

   _____

2. Will Roger try to steal again? Why or why not?

   _____

   _____

   _____

   _____

   _____

3. How does Mrs. Jones demonstrate the importance of taking responsibility?

   _____

   _____

   _____

   _____

   _____

4. How do both Roger and Mrs. Jones act differently than one would initially expect?

   _____

   _____

   _____

   _____

   _____

5. What does the fact that Roger and Mrs. Jones act differently than one might expect teach readers?

   _____

   _____

   _____

   _____

Activity 5. Optional: "Thank You, M'am" - Session 2 *(Online)*

Student Guide
Lesson 3: "The Circuit": Session 1

Today, you will read a story that focuses on the lives of one family of migrant workers and the struggles they endure.

Lesson Objectives
- Identify first-person point of view.
- Recognize author's purpose and devices used to accomplish it, including author's language, organization, and structure.
- Describe characters based on speech, actions, or interactions with others.
- Identify character traits and motivations.
- Recognize use of language to convey mood.

PREPARE

Approximate lesson time is 60 minutes.

Materials
For the Student

Classics for Young Readers, Vol. 6 - pages 268-276

Reading Notebook

Keywords and Pronunciation
first-person point of view : narration of a story by one of the characters, using the first-person pronouns *I* and *me*

mood : the emotions or feelings conveyed in a literary work

protagonist (proh-TAG-uh-nist) : the main character; the character around whom the action of the plot centers

setting : where and when a literary work takes place

LEARN
Activity 1: "The Circuit" - Session 1 *(Online)*

Activity 2: "The Circuit" - Session 1 *(Offline)*

Activity 3: "The Circuit" - Session 1 *(Online)*

Activity 4: Getting to Know the Narrator *(Online)*

Activity 5: The Narrator's Feelings *(Online)*

Activity 6: Familial Relationships *(Offline)*

Instructions

1. What aspects of the lives of the narrator and his family are positive? What examples from the text can you find of these aspects?

    _____

    _____

    _____

    _____

    _____

    What aspects of the lives of the narrator and his family are negative? What examples from the text can you find of these aspects?

    _____

    _____

    _____

    _____

    _____

Student Guide
Lesson 4: "The Circuit": Session 2

Yesterday, you met a young boy who must deal with frequent moves and work hard to help his family survive. Today, explore how the author makes readers care about these characters and their lives.

Lesson Objectives

- Describe characters based on speech, actions, or interactions with others.
- Formulate opinions and personal responses after reading.
- Identify character traits and motivations.
- Identify first-person point of view.
- Identify symbolism.
- Identify theme.
- Recognize author's purpose and devices used to accomplish it, including author's language, organization, and structure.
- Recognize use of dialect.
- Identify climax.
- Identify elements of a short story.
- Recognize use of language to convey mood.

PREPARE

Approximate lesson time is 60 minutes.

Keywords and Pronunciation

plot : what happens in a story; the sequence of events

climax : the point of highest action in a story; the turning point

complicating incident : an important early event that signals that the action is about to start

conflict : a clash or struggle between people, ideas, or feelings; characters can have a conflict within themselves, with another character, with society, or with nature

Exposition : the beginning of a story where the setting, characters, and basic situations are usually introduced

falling action : the part of the plot where issues are resolved and questions are answered

mood : the emotions or feelings conveyed in a literary work

resolution : the solution or working out of a literary conflict

rising action : a series of events that builds interest or suspense

suspense : excitement and uncertainty about what will happen

symbol : something that stands for something else in literature; for example, a dove may be a symbol for peace

theme : the main message that an author wants to communicate to a reader

---

LEARN
Activity 1: "The Circuit" - Session 2 *(Online)*

Activity 2: The Shape and Mood of the Story *(Online)*

Activity 3: Putting It All Together *(Offline)*
Instructions

1. At the start of this story, the narrator describes how much he, his brother, and their father have been working picking strawberries: "twelve hours a day, every day, seven days a week, week after week." Yet on his last day of work, the narrator thinks of how much he will miss the job. Why would he miss such a demanding occupation? What does the final day of the strawberry-picking season signal to him?

   _____
   _____
   _____
   _____

2. What is similar between the narrator's descriptions of how his family packs up their car and how they unpack and move into their home on the Sullivan farm? What can readers learn about the narrator's family from these descriptions?

   _____
   _____
   _____
   _____
   _____

3. The theme of a story is the main message that the author conveys to readers. Think about the events of "The Circuit"--the way in which the characters behave, the circumstances they face, and the events that shape their lives. What message do you think the story conveys?

   _____
   _____
   _____
   _____
   _____
   _____

4. After reading the first part of this story, you answered two questions: one about the positive aspects of the migrant worker's lifestyle and one about the negative aspects of the migrant worker's lifestyle. Now that you have finished the story, do you think the closeness and unity of this family make up for the instability that is such a regular part of their lives? Support your answer.

    _____
    _____
    _____
    _____
    _____
    _____

ASSESS
Lesson Assessment: "The Circuit" - Session 2 (*Online*)
Check your understanding by answering these questions on the first four lessons of this unit.

LEARN
Activity 4. Optional: "The Circuit" - Session 2 *(Online)*

Student Guide
Lesson 5: "The Bracelet": Session 1

What was it like to be Japanese American during World War II, when your home country was fighting the country of your ancestors? Learn about the experiences of one Japanese-American family by reading "The Bracelet," by Yoshiko Uchida.

Lesson Objectives

- Recognize author's purpose and devices used to accomplish it, including author's language, organization, and structure.
- Describe characters based on speech, actions, or interactions with others.
- Identify character traits and motivations.
- Formulate personal responses after reading.
- Identify symbolism.
- Recognize use of language to convey mood.

PREPARE

Approximate lesson time is 60 minutes.

Materials

> For the Student
>> Classics for Young Readers, Vol. 6 - pages 277-280
>> Reading Notebook

Keywords and Pronunciation

mood : the emotions or feelings conveyed in a literary work

symbolism : the literary technique of using something to stand for or represent another idea; for example, a dove frequently symbolizes peace, while a single red rose sometimes symbolizes love

LEARN
Activity 1: "The Bracelet" - Session 1 *(Online)*

Activity 2: "The Bracelet" - Session 1 *(Offline)*

Activity 3: "The Bracelet" - Session 1 *(Online)*

Activity 4: Emptiness (Online)

Activity 5: The Garden (Online)

Activity 6: Thinking More About Ruri (Offline)
Instructions

1. How does Ruri feel about what is happening to her family? How do you know?

   _____

   _____

   _____

2. "The Bracelet" is told from the first-person point of view. How does this affect the story? How does it affect the way readers understand what happens to Ruri?

   _____

   _____

   _____

   _____

   _____

   _____

3. How does the fact that Ruri tells her own story affect the way readers feel about her and her family? Would another point of view be as effective?

   _____

   _____

   _____

   _____

4. If you could speak to Ruri about what she is going through, what would you say?

   _____

   _____

   _____

   _____

   _____

Activity 7. Optional: "The Bracelet" - Session 1 (Online)

Student Guide
Lesson 6: "The Bracelet": Session 2

At the end of yesterday's reading, Ruri and her family were about to be sent to an internment camp. What will the camp be like and how will the family members react? Read the second part of "The Bracelet" and find out.

Lesson Objectives
- Identify the effect of first-person point of view.
- Recognize author's purpose and devices used to accomplish it, including author's language, organization, and structure.
- Describe characters based on speech, actions, or interactions with others.
- Identify character traits and motivations.
- Identify symbolism.
- Identify theme.
- Recognize use of language to convey mood.

PREPARE

Approximate lesson time is 60 minutes.

Materials
> For the Student
>> Classics for Young Readers, Vol. 6 - pages 282-284
>> Reading Notebook

Keywords and Pronunciation
first-person point of view : narration of a story by one of the characters, using the first-person pronouns *I* and *me*
point of view : the perspective from which a story is told

LEARN
Activity 1: "The Bracelet" - Session 2 *(Online)*

Activity 2: "The Bracelet" - Session 2 *(Offline)*

Activity 3: "The Bracelet" - Session 2 *(Online)*

Activity 4: The Apartment *(Online)*

Activity 5: Review and Reflect *(Offline)*
Instructions

1. In what ways is Ruri's mother an important role model for Ruri? What does Ruri's mother teach her daughter?

    _____

    _____

    _____

    _____

    _____

    _____

2. How does telling the story from the **first-person point of view** affect readers' perception of the camps?

    _____

    _____

    _____

    _____

3. How does telling the story from a child's **point of view** help readers grasp just how complex this situation is?

    _____

    _____

    _____

    _____

4. How does knowing that the author was in an interment camp affect your reaction to this story?

    _____

    _____

    _____

    _____

    _____

5. Why might the author have chosen to tell about this experience through fiction rather than nonfiction?

    _____

    _____

    _____

    _____

    _____

    _____

6. What can this story teach a reader? Would you recommend this story and the message it teaches to another reader? Why or why not?

_____

_____

_____

_____

_____

Student Guide
Lesson 7: "The Strangers That Came to Town": Session 1

Lesson Objectives

- Recognize author's purpose and devices used to accomplish it, including author's language, organization, and structure.
- Describe characters based on speech, actions, or interactions with others.
- Identify character traits and motivations.
- Formulate opinions and personal responses after reading.
- Identify conflict and resolution.
- Recognize use of language to convey mood.
- Identify elements of a short story.

PREPARE

Approximate lesson time is 60 minutes.

Materials

For the Student

Classics for Young Readers, Vol. 6 - pages 285-290

Keywords and Pronunciation

conflict : a clash or struggle between people, ideas, or feelings; characters can have a conflict within themselves, with another character, with society, or with nature

rising action : a series of events that builds interest or suspense

stereotype : a generalized or oversimplified view, usually negative, of something or someone

LEARN
Activity 1: "The Strangers That Came to Town" - Session 1 *(Online)*

Activity 2: "The Strangers That Came to Town" - Session 1 *(Offline)*

Activity 3: "The Strangers That Came to Town" - Session 1 *(Online)*

Activity 4: Syringa Street *(Online)*

Activity 5: Father *(Online)*

Activity 6. Optional: "The Strangers That Came to Town" - Session 1 *(Online)*

Student Guide
Lesson 8: "The Strangers That Came to Town": Session 2

Lesson Objectives

- Describe characters based on speech, actions, or interactions with others.
- Identify character traits and motivations.
- Identify climax.
- Identify conflict and resolution.
- Identify elements of a short story.
- Identify symbolism.
- Identify the effect of first-person point of view.
- Identify theme.
- Recognize author's purpose and devices used to accomplish it, including author's language, organization, and structure.
- Recognize use of language to convey mood.
- Recognize devices used by an author to achieve the purpose, including language, organization, or structure.
- Recognize use of dialect.

PREPARE

Approximate lesson time is 60 minutes.

Materials

For the Student

Classics for Young Readers, Vol. 6 - pages 291-296

Keywords and Pronunciation

climax : the point of highest action in a story; the turning point

conflict : a clash or struggle between people, ideas, or feelings; characters can have a conflict within themselves, with another character, with society, or with nature

falling action : the part of the plot where issues are resolved and questions are answered

resolution : the solution or working out of a literary conflict

stereotype : a generalized or oversimplified view, usually negative, of something or someone

LEARN
Activity 1: "The Strangers That Came to Town" - Session 2 *(Online)*

Activity 2: "The Strangers That Came to Town" - Session 2 *(Offline)*

Activity 3: "The Strangers That Came to Town" - Session 2 *(Online)*

Activity 4: Climax, Conflict, and Resolution *(Online)*

ASSESS

Lesson Checkpoint: Stories of Our Time (*Online*)

It's time to check what you have learned. Go to the next screen to test your skills.

Student Guide
Lesson 9: Review and Writing a Literary Essay: Session 1

Congratulations, you have finished the reading for this unit. Today, you will review the major events, characters, and themes of the stories. Then, you will begin preparing to write a literary essay.

Lesson Objectives
- Describe characters based on speech, actions, or interactions with others.
- Identify character traits and motivations.
- Identify theme.
- Use an effective pattern of organization.
- Use and maintain a tone appropriate to the audience and purpose.
- Use transitions to connect ideas.
- Write an essay that contains an introduction, thesis statement, supporting paragraphs, and conclusion.

PREPARE
Approximate lesson time is 60 minutes.

Materials
For the Student

Reading Notebook

⌨ Roger and Mrs. Jones: Expect the Unexpected

Keywords and Pronunciation
chronological order : organizational pattern in which details are arranged in the order they occur

conflict : a clash or struggle between people, ideas, or feelings; characters can have a conflict within themselves, with another character, with society, or with nature

first-person point of view : narration of a story by one of the characters, using the first-person pronouns *I* and *me*

point-by-point structure : an organizing pattern used for comparison and contrast essays in which one feature common to both subjects is compared or contrasted in the same paragraph

theme : the main message that an author wants to communicate to a reader

thesis : the most important point, or main idea, of an essay

LEARN
Activity 1: Major Characters, Events, and Themes Review *(Online)*

Activity 2: Questions (Online)

Activity 3: Discussion Time (Offline)
Instructions
Discuss the following questions in order to better understand the themes of this unit and what the characters learn from their experiences. You may discuss them with another reader or answer the questions in your Reading Notebook.

1. Briefly summarize what Roger, the narrator in "The Circuit," Ruri, and the narrator in "The Strangers That Came to Town" each learn from the events of their respective stories.

2. How is the impact of Langston Hughes's use of **dialect** in "Thank You, M'am" similar to the use of the Spanish language in "The Circuit"?

3. How does the behavior of Ruri's mother in "The Bracelet" serve as a positive example for the young girl to follow?

4. How are Mr. Duvitch and Father similar in "The Strangers That Came to Town"? What does this similarity suggest?

5. Which stories in this unit employ the **first-person point of view?** How does this point of view affect readers?

Activity 4: Literary Essay - Responding as a Reader (Online)

Model Essay

Roger and Mrs. Jones: Expect the Unexpected
by Ken Carmine

Consider this situation as the starting point of a story: it is late at night, and a young boy tries to steal the purse of an old woman as she walks home. Is there anything original or unusual about this situation? If this were just a crime story, the answer would be "no," but author Langston Hughes turns an attempted mugging into a short story that shows how one woman demonstrates her generosity, kindness, and compassion to a troubled boy. "Thank You, M'am" is a memorable and moving story about two characters, Mrs. Luella Bates Washington Jones and Roger, who are both far more complex and surprising than most readers ever expect.

From the very beginning of the story, Mrs. Jones surprises readers. Rather than allowing herself to be the victim of a mugging, she resists Roger and turns the tables on him. She takes charge. She kicks Roger in the seat of his pants and holds him tightly so that he cannot run away. She then yells at the boy for what he has tried to do and brings him back to her home. This is certainly not what most readers would expect from an old woman. Mrs. Jones's behavior indicates that she is not only physically strong, but that she also has a strong character. She is clearly not a person who will back down from any challenge or problem. Readers are immediately interested to see what she will do with Roger and wonder why she is bringing him home with her.

However, as surprising as the behavior of Mrs. Jones is, Roger's behavior is equally unexpected. Most readers would suppose that a young person who is daring and thoughtless enough to attempt to rob an old woman would be brash and rude. At the very least, readers expect Roger to be unafraid of a woman like Mrs. Jones. However, when Mrs. Jones fights back against Roger, he is quite frightened and timid. He even begs Mrs. Jones to let him go. He says, "I just want you to turn me loose," as she drags him down the street. By the time Mrs. Jones brings Roger back to her apartment, it is clear that she is in total control of the situation. Readers now want to see how this odd pair behaves as the story progresses. The unusual nature of both characters has captured reader attention fully.

In Mrs. Jones's apartment, the characters continue to act in unexpected and surprising ways. One might assume that Mrs. Jones brings Roger with her to lecture him or punish him for what he has done, but she instead offers to make him dinner. Rather than tell him that she would never do anything as shameful as what Roger has done, Mrs. Jones admits that she too has done things of which she is not proud. This confession not only makes readers realize how honest Mrs. Jones is, it also has an impact on Roger. Because Mrs. Jones shows that she trusts him, Roger behaves not as a thief, but like a young man who deserves to be trusted. He does not steal from her purse when Mrs. Jones's back is turned, and he

Model Essay

even offers to go to the store to do some shopping for Mrs. Jones. Mrs. Jones's pride and dignity affect Roger. They make him behave better.

By the end of "Thank You, M'am," readers have had nearly every expectation they held about Roger and Mrs. Jones proven to be incorrect. The woman who seems as if she would be an easy target and likely victim turns out to be a strong and generous figure who refuses to judge others. The heartless thief who preys on seemingly defenseless individuals turns out to be a scared and neglected young person in need of guidance. By showing that these characters are so different from how they first appear to be, author Langston Hughes reminds readers what strength really is and that people should never be judged on appearances only.

Student Guide
Lesson 10: Writing a Literary Essay: Session 2

Yesterday, you read a model literary essay and answered several questions on it. Today, you will complete a pre-writing assignment designed to help you choose a topic for your literary essay and begin taking notes on that topic.

Lesson Objectives

- Describe characters based on speech, actions, or interactions with others.
- Identify character traits and motivations.
- Identify theme.
- Use an effective pattern of organization.
- Use and maintain a tone appropriate to the audience and purpose.
- Use transitions to connect ideas.
- Write an essay that contains an introduction, thesis statement, supporting paragraphs, and conclusion.

PREPARE

Approximate lesson time is 60 minutes.

Materials

For the Student

- Preparing to Write - Literary Essay
- Preparing to Write - Model
- Questions for Topic 1
- Questions for Topic 2
- Questions for Topic 3

Keywords and Pronunciation

brainstorming : a prewriting technique in which the writer tries to come up with as many ideas as possible without judging them

chronological order : organizational pattern in which details are arranged in the order they occur

logical order : organizational pattern in which details are grouped together such as in comparison and contrast, where the similarities or differences are grouped together

theme : the main message that an author wants to communicate to a reader

thesis : the most important point, or main idea, of an essay

tone : the writer's attitude toward the topic or subject

LEARN
Activity 1: Choosing a Topic, Taking Notes, and Organizing (Offline)
Instructions
A: Choosing a Topic

The first decision that a writer must make before beginning an essay is choosing what to write about. Many possible topics may come to mind when you are **brainstorming**, but not all will be appropriate or will lend themselves to exploration in a literary essay. Some topics may be too simple and others may be too complex. For this assignment, you will choose between two basic types of essays:

- An essay that focuses on what a character learns over the course of a story

- An essay that focuses on a particular theme in a story

An example of the first type of essay would be one that explores what Ruri learns from her mother and her family's experiences in "The Bracelet." An example of the second type of essay would be one that focuses on the idea of acceptance in "The Strangers That Came to Town." Of course, in order to discuss **theme,** you will need to discuss the characters and what they learn. And if your exploration of the experiences of characters and what they learn leads to a theme, you may discuss that as well.

Your own interests should guide you in choosing your essay topic. The more interested you are in the topic, the more you will enjoy writing about it. To choose your topic for this specific assignment, consider the following questions. Discuss these questions in order to help yourself narrow down your options and finally make a choice.

- In writing your essay, you will have to work closely with one of the stories from this unit. Which story interested you the most in this unit? Why?

- Some of the essay options require you to focus closely on certain characters. Which characters in this unit did you like most or care most about? Why?

- Some of the essay options ask you to explore themes. Which themes in this unit mean the most to you? Why?

Choose your literary essay topic from one of the following:

1. How do the events of "The Strangers That Came to Town" teach the narrator a lesson about judging others and acceptance?

2. Discuss how the family in "The Circuit" demonstrates the importance of teamwork and unity throughout that story.

3. What does Ruri learn from her mother and her experiences in "The Bracelet"?

Consider which of these topics deals with the stories, characters, and themes that you are most interested in. Tomorrow you will begin preparing your literary essay. Now, print the Topic Questions page that goes with the essay topic you have selected. You will only need to answer questions for your chosen topic.

B: Taking Notes

Now that you know the topic of your essay, the following steps will help you take notes.

1. Think about what type of essay you are writing. Are you exploring what a character learns in a story? Are you examining how a theme develops in a story?

2. Go back and reread the story that will be central to your essay. As you read, keep your topic in mind and look for textual evidence that supports the points you will try to make.

3. When you find parts of the text that relate to your topic, take notes detailing where you found them and how you might use them in your essay.

4. Once you have reread the story that is important to your essay and taken notes, review those notes and consider how your arguments will fit together.

You've already covered the first point above, so you are ready to move on to the next three steps.

The first step in writing about a story is to go back and reread the text. While rereading, you should take notes and begin to find textual evidence that relates to your topic.

Remember the following tips on good note-taking:

- Note all textual details that you intend to use in relation to your topic. Keep track of where these details appear by including page numbers where appropriate.

- Note important quotations that relate to your topic. When copying quotations, be sure that you write them down exactly as they appear in the text.

- Organize your notes in the same basic shape that you plan on having your essay take.

- Group related facts and ideas together.

- Include thoughts that you have while taking notes if you think they will help you as you begin outlining and writing.

As is always the case with taking notes, you do not need to write complete or grammatically correct sentences. Just make sure that you write your notes in a way that they will be meaningful and helpful to you later.

Before you start taking notes for your literary essay, print and read the Preparing to Write--Model and the Preparing to Write--Literary Essay pages. The model page provides an example of the initial steps of pre-writing. Read over the model and then follow its example when taking notes for your literary essay.

C: Patterns of Organization for a Literary Essay

Now that you have taken notes on your topic, you can begin thinking about how you will organize your ideas and shape your essay.

Literary essays can take several different forms. Some essays, like Ken's essay on Roger and Mrs. Jones, describe events as they occur chronologically through a story. Others deal with issues and events from different parts of a story in order to make a point. Still others focus on issues in order of importance. How you choose to shape your work is largely dependent on the type of essay you are writing. The thing to remember is that your essay should flow together logically. That is, the ideas in your essay should connect in a way that makes sense. On the following pages you will see a few examples of the different shapes that your essay may take.

Chronological Order

If you are writing an essay that explores how a theme develops over the course of a story, it may make sense to follow the **chronological order** of the story in your essay. Examine how the major **theme** is expressed at the beginning, middle, and end of the story. Here is an example of the basic layout for this type of essay. For this example, suppose that the essay focuses on the importance of friendship to a character.

I. Introduction
II. Body Paragraph 1--Discuss the importance of friendship at the start of the story. Include textual evidence to support your ideas.
III. Body Paragraph 2--Explore the importance of friendship in the middle of the story. Discuss how the role of friendship has changed. Include textual evidence to support your ideas.
IV.Body Paragraph 3--Examine the importance of friendship at the end of the story. Show how the role of friendship has continued to change. Include textual evidence to support your ideas.
V. Conclusion

However, if you are writing an essay about how a character changes in a story, you may not want to delay showing your reader the change in the character. Perhaps it makes sense to begin with how the character is at the story's end and then shift to how the character was at the beginning. Here is an example of how that essay's layout might look.

I. Introduction

II. Body Paragraph 1--Discuss the character at the end of the story. Provide examples from the text to support your ideas.

III. Body Paragraph 2--Return to the beginning to show how the character was at the start of the story. Provide examples from the text to support your ideas and show the differences.

IV.Body Paragraph 3--Explore the middle of the story and the events that changed the character. Include textual evidence to support your ideas.

V. Conclusion

Order of Importance

Another way to organize a literary essay is to present your ideas in the order in which they seem important to you. You may go from most important to least important, as in the following model:

I. Introduction

II. Body Paragraph 1--Identification of most important idea, supported by details

III. Body Paragraph 2--Identification of second most important idea, supported by details

IV.Body Paragraph 3--Identification of third most important idea, supported by details

V. Conclusion

Or, you may build order of importance from the least important to the most important idea, as in the following example:

I. Introduction

II. Body Paragraph 1--Identification of third most important idea, supported by details

III. Body Paragraph 2--Identification of second most important idea, supported by details

IV. Body Paragraph 3--Identification of most important idea, supported by details

V. Conclusion

You now have some ideas about how a literary essay can be organized. In the next lesson, you will organize your essay by making an outline. To guide you in structuring your outline, you will write a **thesis statement** that sums up the main idea of the essay. Notes, a thesis statement, and an outline--these foundations will make it much easier for you when you come to the actual drafting of the essay in Lesson 12.

Name _____   Date _____

Literary Essay

Preparing to Write – Literary Essay

Follow the example of the model page as you fill in the spaces below. After you've finished, save this page for use tomorrow.

Topic: _____

_____

Short summary of the story: _____

_____

_____

_____

Notes during reread of the story:

_____

_____

_____

_____

_____

_____

_____

_____

_____

_____

_____

_____

_____

_____

_____

_____

_____

_____

Model Essay

Discuss the effect of the behavior of Mrs. Jones and Roger in "Thank You, M'am."

These are some of the notes that Ken Carmine took while preparing his literary essay. Save this page for tomorrow.

Short summary of the story: Roger is a young would-be thief who tries to mug Mrs. Jones. Rather than be a victim, Mrs. Jones grabs Roger and brings him back to her home. There, she cleans the boy up and shares a meal with him. When she finds out that he tried to rob her so that he could buy a pair of shoes, she does not lecture him. Instead, she says that she too has done things that are wrong. As the story ends, Mrs. Jones gives Roger the money to buy the shoes and warns him not to steal anymore. Roger is so overcome by her kindness that he can only mouth the words "Thank you, M'am" as the story ends.

Notes during reread of the story:

- Both Mrs. Jones and Roger act in ways that are unexpected. This interests readers and makes them take a closer look at these characters. What is the author telling us? Don't judge.

- Mrs. Jones is an old woman, seems like a likely victim. Most readers would think that she would be weak and frail and not confrontational. Roger tries to rob her. She fights back. Pages 262-263: she kicks him and grabs him and won't let him go. She yells at him for what he's done. She is not only stronger than the boy; she has a stronger personality. She is in control of the situation.

- Roger is a young boy, would-be thief. But he is not bold or brash. He seems timid. Not what one would expect from a person who tries to mug an old woman. It is as if Roger and Mrs. Jones are in opposite roles. He is scared of Mrs. Jones. Begs her to let him go. Page 263: "I just want you to turn me loose" as he is being dragged down the street.

- Back at the apartment, the surprises continue. Pages 264-265: Mrs. Jones does not lecture or punish Roger. Instead, she treats him well. She has him wash his face and tells him that she too has made mistakes. This makes Roger feel comfortable. She is not judging him. All of this is surprising. Roger, in turn, decides that he wants to be trusted.

- Mrs. Jones cooks for herself and Roger. Roger offers to go to the store to help Mrs. Jones. The two share a meal. Pages 265-266.

- Things are not what they seem in this story. Every expectation is proven incorrect by these characters who behave in ways that are unexpected. This helps readers to understand what the author is saying about making assumptions.

Name _____   Date _____

Topic 1: How do the events of "The Strangers That Came to Town" teach the narrator a lesson about judging others and acceptance?

Questions to consider:

1. What characters in this story are judged by others and are seeking acceptance?

   _____

   _____

2. How are the characters who are judged depicted?

   _____

   _____

   _____

   _____

   _____

3. How are those characters who judge others and deny acceptance to others depicted?

   _____

   _____

   _____

4. What events in the story help the narrator learn about judging others and acceptance?

   _____

   _____

   _____

   _____

   _____

Name _____   Date _____

Topic 2: Discuss how the family in "The Circuit" demonstrates the importance of teamwork and unity throughout that story.

Questions to consider:

1. Why are teamwork and unity valuable to groups of people?

   _____

   _____

   _____

2. How does the family in this story benefit from teamwork and unity?

   _____

   _____

   _____

3. What examples from the story demonstrate these benefits?

   _____

   _____

   _____

   _____

   _____

Name _____ **Date** _____

Topic 3: What does Ruri learn from her mother and her experiences in "The Bracelet"?

Questions to consider:

1. What experiences does Ruri have in "The Bracelet"?

   _____

   _____

   _____

2. How do these experiences make Ruri feel?

   _____

   _____

   _____

3. How does Ruri's mother react to the events of the story?

   _____

   _____

   _____

4. What effect does Ruri's mother have on her?

   _____

   _____

   _____

Student Guide
Lesson 11: Writing a Literary Essay: Session 3

Yesterday, you took notes on the work from this unit that will be the focus of your literary essay. You also learned about several possible ways of organizing a literary essay. Today, you will create a thesis statement to sum up your ideas on your topic. That statement, and your notes, will form the basis of an outline from which you will build your essay.

Lesson Objectives

- Describe characters based on speech, actions, or interactions with others.
- Identify character traits and motivations.
- Identify theme.
- Write an essay that contains an introduction, thesis statement, supporting paragraphs, and conclusion.
- Use an effective pattern of organization.
- Use transitions to connect ideas.
- Use and maintain a tone appropriate to the audience and purpose.

PREPARE

Approximate lesson time is 60 minutes.

Materials

For the Student

household items - Different colored highlighters or pens

⌨ Outline - Literary Essay

⌨ Outline - Model

Keywords and Pronunciation

chronological order : organizational pattern in which details are arranged in the order they occur

thesis statement : the sentence that states the main idea of an essay

LEARN
Activity 1: Creating a Thesis Statement *(Online)*

Activity 2: Getting Your Ideas in Order *(Online)*

Activity 3: Organizing Your Ideas - Building an Outline (Offline)
Instructions

An outline is the skeleton of an essay--it should contain the important ideas and facts that will support your essay's arguments. It should show the basic shape that the essay will take. For this essay, you will construct an outline with five sections. These five sections will correspond to the five paragraphs of your essay. The sections are as follows:

I. Introduction (with thesis statement)
II. Supporting Evidence--Part 1 (with topic sentence)
III. Supporting Evidence--Part 2 (with topic sentence)
IV. Supporting Evidence--Part 3 (with topic sentence)
V. Conclusion (with restatement of thesis)

In each of these sections of your outline, you will fill in the major facts that will make up the body of your essay.

Here are a few hints for using your pre-writing notes to create an effective and useful outline:

- In your introduction, state your thesis. Also provide background for your reader by reviewing major facts about the work that are related to your thesis.
- Be sure that the topic sentence of each body paragraph supports your thesis and provides a main idea for that paragraph.
- Choose appropriate supporting details in your notes, and find places where they fit into your supporting paragraphs. Think of it as like putting together a jigsaw puzzle.
- Conclude by summarizing the points you've made in the body of the essay and restating your thesis.

In order to see how a full outline should look, read the Outline--Model page and examine how it developed from the Preparing to Write--Model page.

Now it's your turn to develop an outline. Follow the directions to complete the Outline--Literary Essay page.

Use your Preparing to Write--Literary Essay page to build an outline into the framework provided. Feel free to use the model outline as an example from which to work. Good luck!

Name _____   Date _____

Outline – Literary Essay

Use your Preparing to Write – Literary Essay page to build an outline into the framework below. Feel free to use the model outline as an example from which to work. Good luck!

Topic: _____

_____

I.   Introduction
      A. Background Information – _____

_____

_____

      B. Thesis Statement – _____

_____

_____

II.   Supporting Evidence, Part 1
      A. Topic Sentence – _____

_____

_____

      B. Evidence from the text – _____

_____

_____

      C. Evidence from the text – _____

_____

_____

      D. Evidence from the text – _____

_____

_____

III.   Supporting Evidence, Part 2
      A. Topic Sentence – _____

_____

_____

Name _____   Date _____

B. Evidence from the text – _____

_____

_____

C. Evidence from the text – _____

_____

_____

D. Evidence from the text – _____

_____

_____

IV.   Supporting Evidence, Part 3
      A. Topic Sentence – _____

_____

_____

B. Evidence from the text – _____

_____

_____

C. Evidence from the text – _____

_____

_____

D. Evidence from the text – _____

_____

_____

V.   Conclusion
      A. Summary of points made in essay – _____

_____

_____

B. Restatement of thesis – _____

_____

_____

Outline – Model

Here is Ken Carmine's outline for his literary essay. You may want to use it as a model for your own outline. Save this page for tomorrow.

Topic: Discuss the effect of the behavior of Mrs. Jones and Roger in "Thank You, M'am."

I.   Introduction

A. Brief description of story's plot – A young boy snatches the purse from an old woman. The behavior of each character is surprising and shows the reader that these characters are much more complicated and surprising than expected.

B. Thesis Statement – "Thank You, M'am" is a memorable and moving story about two characters, Mrs. Luella Bates Washington Jones and Roger, who are both far more complex and surprising than most readers ever expect.

II.   Supporting Evidence, Part 1 – *The ideas in this section all come from the beginning of the story. The topic sentence is the main idea of the paragraph.*

A. Topic Sentence – From the very beginning of the story, Mrs. Jones surprises readers.

B. Evidence from the text – Mrs. Jones refuses to be a victim.

C. Evidence from the text – She kicks Roger, yells at him, grabs him, and refuses to let go.

D. Evidence from the text – She's physically stronger and her personality is stronger. She is in total control of the situation. All of this is not what readers would generally expect from an old woman.

III.   Supporting Evidence, Part 2 – *The ideas in this section all come from slightly later in the story. The topic sentence is the main idea of the paragraph and moves the essay forward.*

A. Topic Sentence – However, as surprising as the behavior of Mrs. Jones is, Roger's behavior is equally unexpected.

B. Evidence from the text – Roger tries to rob Mrs. Jones, which is brash and rude, but he acts quite differently from this when caught.

C. Evidence from the text – Roger is scared and timid. He begs Mrs. Jones to let him go (page 263).

D. Evidence from the text – Roger is not in control of the situation at all; he is clearly the weaker of the two characters, both physically and in terms of his personality.

IV.   Supporting Evidence, Part 3 – *The ideas in this section come from the latter part of the story. The topic sentence is the main idea of the paragraph.*

A. Topic Sentence – In Mrs. Jones's apartment, the characters continue to act in unexpected and surprising ways.

B. Evidence from the text – Mrs. Jones does not lecture Roger. She cleans him up, admits that she's done things of which she is ashamed.

C. Evidence from the text – Roger begins to feel more comfortable, wants to be trusted, even offers to go to the store for Mrs. Jones.

D. Evidence from the text – The two characters eat together, certainly not what readers would have expected…the would-be mugger eating with his victim.

V.   Conclusion – *The conclusion summarizes the points made by restating the main points (drawn from the topic sentences) and restating the thesis.*

A. Summary of points made in essay – Mrs. Jones is strong and in control. Roger is weak and in need of guidance. The characters continually act in surprising ways.

B. Restatement of thesis – By showing that these characters are so different from how they first appear to be, Langston Hughes creates a memorable and moving story that reminds readers that it is impossible to judge a book by its cover.

Student Guide
Lesson 12: Writing a Literary Essay: Session 4

Lesson Objectives

- Describe characters based on speech, actions, or interactions with others.
- Identify character traits and motivations.
- Identify theme.
- Use an effective pattern of organization.
- Use and maintain a tone appropriate to the audience and purpose.
- Use complete sentences and correct capitalization, punctuation, and spelling.
- Use transitions to connect ideas.
- Write an essay that contains an introduction, thesis statement, supporting paragraphs, and conclusion.

PREPARE

Approximate lesson time is 60 minutes.

Materials

For the Student

    📖 Literary Essay - Model

Keywords and Pronunciation

clarity : when writing is clear and easy to understand

conclusion : the final paragraph of an essay

first-person point of view : narration of a story by one of the characters, using the first-person pronouns *I* and *me*

hook : a surprising or intriguing passage, idea, or image used to grab the reader's attention, usually at the beginning of a work

introduction : the first paragraph of an essay, identifying the topic and stating the main idea

style : the words the writer chooses and the way the writer arranges the words into sentences

thesis : the most important point, or main idea, of an essay

tone : the writer's attitude toward the topic or subject

topic sentence : the sentence that expresses the main idea of the paragraph

transition : a word or phrase that connects ideas

unity : a trait of writing achieved when all sentences in a paragraph or all paragraphs in an essay support the main idea

LEARN
Activity 1: From Outline to Draft *(Online)*

Activity 2: The First Draft - Tone, Transitions, and Style *(Online)*

Model Essay

Roger and Mrs. Jones: Expect the Unexpected
by Ken Carmine

Consider this situation as the starting point of a story: it is late at night, and a young boy tries to steal the purse of an old woman as she walks home. Is there anything original or unusual about this situation? If this were just a crime story, the answer would be "no," but author Langston Hughes turns an attempted mugging into a short story that shows how one woman demonstrates her generosity, kindness, and compassion to a troubled boy. "Thank You, M'am" is a memorable and moving story about two characters, Mrs. Luella Bates Washington Jones and Roger, who are both far more complex and surprising than most readers ever expect.

From the very beginning of the story, Mrs. Jones surprises readers. Rather than allowing herself to be the victim of a mugging, she resists Roger and turns the tables on him. She takes charge. She kicks Roger in the seat of his pants and holds him tightly so that he cannot run away. She then yells at the boy for what he has tried to do and brings him back to her home. This is certainly not what most readers would expect from an old woman. Mrs. Jones's behavior indicates that she is not only physically strong, but that she also has a strong character. She is clearly not a person who will back down from any challenge or problem. Readers are immediately interested to see what she will do with Roger and wonder why she is bringing him home with her.

However, as surprising as the behavior of Mrs. Jones is, Roger's behavior is equally unexpected. Most readers would suppose that a young person who is daring and thoughtless enough to attempt to rob an old woman would be brash and rude. At the very least, readers expect Roger to be unafraid of a woman like Mrs. Jones. However, when Mrs. Jones fights back against Roger, he is quite frightened and timid. He even begs Mrs. Jones to let him go. He says, "I just want you to turn me loose," as she drags him down the street. By the time Mrs. Jones brings Roger back to her apartment, it is clear that she is in total control of the situation. Readers now want to see how this odd pair behaves as the story progresses. The unusual nature of both characters has captured reader attention fully.

In Mrs. Jones's apartment, the characters continue to act in unexpected and surprising ways. One might assume that Mrs. Jones brings Roger with her to lecture him or punish him for what he has done, but she instead offers to make him dinner. Rather than tell him that she would never do anything as shameful as what Roger has done, Mrs. Jones admits that she too has done things of which she is not proud. This confession not only makes readers realize how honest Mrs. Jones is, it also has an impact on Roger. Because Mrs. Jones shows that she trusts him, Roger behaves not as a thief, but like a young man who deserves to be trusted. He does not steal from her purse when Mrs. Jones's back is turned, and he

Model Essay

even offers to go to the store to do some shopping for Mrs. Jones. Mrs. Jones's pride and dignity affect Roger. They make him behave better.

By the end of "Thank You, M'am," readers have had nearly every expectation they held about Roger and Mrs. Jones proven to be incorrect. The woman who seems as if she would be an easy target and likely victim turns out to be a strong and generous figure who refuses to judge others. The heartless thief who preys on seemingly defenseless individuals turns out to be a scared and neglected young person in need of guidance. By showing that these characters are so different from how they first appear to be, author Langston Hughes reminds readers what strength really is and that people should never be judged on appearances only.

Student Guide
Lesson 13: Writing a Literary Essay: Session 5

Now that you have completed a rough draft of your literary essay, you will review some strategies for revising and polishing it into a finished product.

Lesson Objectives

- Describe characters based on speech, actions, or interactions with others.
- Identify character traits and motivations.
- Identify theme.
- Revise, proofread, and publish an essay.
- Use an effective pattern of organization.
- Use and maintain a tone appropriate to the audience and purpose.
- Use complete sentences and correct capitalization, punctuation, and spelling.
- Use transitions to connect ideas.
- Write an essay that contains an introduction, thesis statement, supporting paragraphs, and conclusion.

PREPARE

Approximate lesson time is 60 minutes.

Materials

For the Student

💻 Checklist for Revising and Proofreading a Literary

LEARN
Activity 1: Revising, Proofreading, and Publishing Your Essay *(Offline)*
Instructions
A. Revising

With your rough draft complete, you are now ready to revise your essay. As you revise, you will make sure that your essay is organized logically, states its ideas clearly, and reads smoothly. Use the Checklist for Revising and Proofreading a Literary Essay to help improve your draft. After completing the first portion of the checklist, return to your draft and make all necessary changes.

B. Proofreading

Use the second part of the checklist to help you proofread your literary essay.

C. Publishing

Now that you have finished writing, revising, correcting, and proofreading your literary essay, you have a polished draft. Congratulations! But what can be done with such an essay?

Consider other people who would be interested in the content of your essay. Feel free to share your work with these people. Perhaps you could begin a literary magazine of your own in which you publish this essay and future works that you and others will write.

ASSESS

Write Now: Stories of Our Time (*Offline*)

It's time to publish your writing. When you've finished polishing your writing, your Learning Coach will review your work and enter the results online.

Name _____   Date _____

Checklist for Revising and Proofreading a Literary Essay

Questions for Revision

☐ Did I explore character traits and motivations by describing what the characters did, said, or how they interacted with others?

If not, how can I add these details?

_____

_____

_____

☐ Did I identify and discuss a theme of the literary work I wrote about?

If not, where should I discuss this idea?

_____

_____

_____

☐ Did I begin with an introduction that contains a strong thesis statement?

If not, how can I improve it?

_____

_____

_____

☐ Have I presented my ideas in a logical order?

If not, how might I present them more logically?

_____

_____

_____

☐ Did I use transitional words and phrases to make the ideas flow together smoothly?

If not, where can I add transitions?

_____

_____

_____

☐ Do my topic sentences clearly support my thesis?

If not, which topic sentences should I change?

_____

_____

_____

☐ Did I use textual evidence to support each topic sentence?

If not, where can I find additional evidence?

_____

_____

_____

Name _____ Date _____

☐ Do all my arguments make sense?   If not, what should I change?

_____

_____

_____

☐ Is the tone consistent and appropriate for my audience?   If not, what changes should I make?

_____

_____

_____

Questions for Proofreading

Place a check in the box next to each question that you can answer "yes" to. If you cannot answer "yes," return to your essay and make the necessary corrections.

☐ Have I indented every paragraph?

☐ Does each sentence in my essay express a complete thought?

☐ Have I capitalized everything in my essay correctly?

☐ Have I titled my essay appropriately and capitalized the title correctly?

☐ Have I used the appropriate punctuation at all times in my essay?

☐ Have I corrected any misspellings and looked up those words of whose spelling I am unsure?

Student Guide
Lesson 1: "Waiting" and "Something Told the Wild Geese"

Lesson Objectives

- Identify and interpret the use of figurative language.
- Recognize use of language to convey mood.
- Compare and contrast literary characters and selections.
- Identify alliteration.
- Contribute meaningfully to group discussions by being prepared for discussion, drawing on preparation, explaining own ideas, building upon others' comments, and asking questions.

PREPARE

Approximate lesson time is 60 minutes.

Advance Preparation

- In the next unit, students will have the opportunity to select a novel to
- read and then complete the associated lessons. Review the list of novels and
- obtain a copy of the desired book. Some novels contain content that may be
- sensitive for some users. Please check the Course Introduction for more
- information.

Materials

For the Student

MLA Handbook for Writers of Research Papers - MLA (Modern Language Association) Full citation: MLA Handbook for Writers of Research Papers. 7th ed. New York: MLA, 2009. Print.

Classics for Young Readers, Vol. 6 - pages 298-299

Reading Notebook

Optional

📖 Guidelines for Peer Discussion

Keywords and Pronunciation

alliteration : the use of words with the same or similar beginning sounds

figurative language : language that uses figures of speech such as metaphor, simile, and personification for poetic effect rather than for precise, factual meaning; for example, "Her eyes are like stars" is figurative language, in contrast to the literal use of "stars" in "The stars are shining tonight"

image : a picture evoked from the words in a piece of writing

imagery : language that creates a mental picture by appealing to the senses, that makes readers see, hear, smell, taste, or feel things in their imagination; for example, "the coal-black night," "the stinging cold," "the rapping and tapping of rain on the roof"

mood : the emotions or feelings conveyed in a literary work

LEARN

Activity 1: "Waiting" and "Something Told the Wild Geese" *(Online)*

Activity 2: "Waiting" and "Something Told the Wild Geese" *(Offline)*

Activity 3: "Waiting" and "Something Told the Wild Geese" *(Online)*

Activity 4: Eye on Language *(Online)*

Activity 5: Two Depictions of Winter *(Online)*

Activity 6: Peer Discussion *(Offline)*

Guidelines for Peer Discussion

Share your thoughts, ideas, questions, and feelings about a text with a peer or others. Listen carefully to what everyone has to say about the text. During your discussion, follow these guidelines.

1. Be prepared to discuss your ideas about the text and to ask and answer questions about what you read. Whenever possible, use examples from the text to support your statements, help others understand your meaning, and justify your answers.

2. Listen carefully and quietly if it's not your turn to speak. Pay attention to what others say so that you can add your ideas. Speak clearly and in complete sentences.

3. Connect and add to the ideas that others have stated using sentences that begin with phrases such as:

   "I understand . . . ."
   "I feel that . . . ."
   "We should also think about how . . . ."
   "That idea relates to . . . ."

4. Respectfully question the opinions of others and politely defend your reasoning if your opinion differs. Use sentences that begin with phrases such as:

   "What do you mean when you say . . .?"
   "Can you give an example of . . .?"
   "I see what you're saying, but what about . . .?"
   "I reacted to that a little differently because . . . ."
   "I disagree with that because . . . ."

5. Draw conclusions about what has already happened in a text and make inferences about what may happen next.

6. Keep the goal(s) of the discussion in mind and respect others. Remember that each member of the group has a valuable contribution to make.

7. Remember that opinions are neither right nor wrong, only different. Remain cordial, thoughtful, and courteous when disagreements or differences of opinion occur.

Student Guide
Lesson 2: "Do You Want to Write Haiku?"

Lesson Objectives

- Identify characteristics of haiku.
- Compare and contrast literary characters and selections.
- Identify and interpret the use of figurative language.
- Recognize use of language to convey mood.

PREPARE

Approximate lesson time is 60 minutes.

Materials

For the Student

Believing Our Ears & Eyes - pages 11-13

Keywords and Pronunciation

dialect : a way of speaking that is particular to a certain group of people, place, or time

mood : the emotions or feelings conveyed in a literary work

speaker : the imaginary person who speaks the words of a poem, not the poet

universal theme : an idea or question that has appeared in many cultures' literature throughout history

---

LEARN
Activity 1: "Do You Want to Write Haiku?" *(Online)*

Activity 2: "Do You Want to Write Haiku?" *(Offline)*

Activity 3: "Do You Want to Write Haiku?" *(Online)*

Activity 4: Season Words *(Online)*

Activity 5: Basho and Issa *(Online)*

Activity 6: More About Haiku *(Online)*

Student Guide
Lesson 3: Six Haiku

Lesson Objectives

- Identify characteristics of haiku.
- Compare and contrast literary characters and selections.
- Identify and interpret the use of figurative language.
- Identify speaker.
- Recognize use of language to convey mood.

PREPARE

Approximate lesson time is 60 minutes.

Materials

For the Student

Classics for Young Readers, Vol. 6 - pages 300-301

Classics for Young Readers, Vol. 6: An Audio Companion - track 11

Keywords and Pronunciation

image : a picture evoked from the words in a piece of writing

imagery : language that creates a mental picture by appealing to the senses, that makes readers see, hear, smell, taste, or feel things in their imagination; for example, "the coal-black night," "the stinging cold," "the rapping and tapping of rain on the roof"

mood : the emotions or feelings conveyed in a literary work

speaker : the imaginary person who speaks the words of a poem, not the poet

symbol : something that stands for something else in literature; for example, a dove may be a symbol for peace

theme : the main message that an author wants to communicate to a reader

LEARN
Activity 1: Six Haiku (Online)

Activity 2: Six Haiku (Offline)

Activity 3: Six Haiku (Online)

Activity 4: Listen Up (Online)

Activity 5: Analyzing the Haiku (Online)

Activity 6. Optional: Six Haiku (Online)

Student Guide
Lesson 4: "The Pasture," "A Wintry Sonnet," and "The Morns Are Meeker..."

Yesterday, you focused on how a traditional Japanese form of poetry uses the seasons to depict important ideas. Now turn your attention to two American poets and one English poet--Emily Dickinson, Robert Frost, and Christina Rossetti--who also set their work against the backdrop of the natural world.

Lesson Objectives

- Compare and contrast literary characters and selections.
- Identify theme.
- Identify and interpret the use of figurative language.
- Identify personification.
- Recognize use of language to convey mood.

PREPARE

Approximate lesson time is 60 minutes.

Materials

> For the Student
>
> > Classics for Young Readers, Vol. 6 - pages 303-305
> >
> > Classics for Young Readers, Vol. 6: An Audio Companion - tracks 13-15

Keywords and Pronunciation

image : a picture evoked from the words in a piece of writing

imagery : language that creates a mental picture by appealing to the senses, that makes readers see, hear, smell, taste, or feel things in their imagination; for example, "the coal-black night," "the stinging cold," "the rapping and tapping of rain on the roof"

meter : the arrangement of words in poetry based on rhythm, accents, and the number of syllables in a line

mood : the emotions or feelings conveyed in a literary work

personification : giving human qualities to a thing or abstraction; for example, "The kettle sang on the hearth," or "After the victory, freedom held its head high in the nation."

speaker : the imaginary person who speaks the words of a poem, not the poet

theme : the main message that an author wants to communicate to a reader

universal theme : an idea or question that has appeared in many cultures' literature throughout history

LEARN
Activity 1: "The Pasture," "A Wintry Sonnet," and "The Morns Are Meeker..."
(Online)

Activity 2: "The Pasture," "A Wintry Sonnet," and "The Morns Are Meeker..."
(Offline)

Activity 3: "The Pasture," "A Wintry Sonnet," and "The Morns Are Meeker..."
(Online)

Activity 4: Frost and Rossetti *(Online)*

Activity 5: Emily Dickinson *(Offline)*
Instructions
With all of her descriptions, Emily Dickinson paints a picture of nature in the fall. Like Frost, she uses language that captures the delicate beauty of the natural world. Like Rossetti, she focuses on several aspects of the natural world and includes language that definitively sets the poem in a particular season.

1. Why does the poet say that the mornings in the fall are milder (meeker) than they were?

   _____

   _____

2. Why are the nuts getting brown?

   _____

   _____

3. Dickinson writes that "berry's cheek is plumper." What does this image suggest?

   _____

   _____

4. What does the line the "Rose is out of town" mean?

   _____

   _____

5. "The Morns Are Meeker Than They Were" is not the only poem in this unit that takes place during the late summer or early fall. You'll recall that "Something Told the Wild Geese" on page 299 is also set during this time of the year. Return to that poem and reread it. Compare and contrast the two poems. How are the depictions of the season similar? How are they different? What themes does each poem address?

_____

_____

_____

_____

_____

_____

Activity 6. Optional: "The Pasture," "A Wintry Sonnet," and "The Morns Are Meeker..." (Online)

Student Guide
Lesson 5: "The Storm" and "Swift Things Are Beautiful"

Continue your exploration of how poetry captures the beauty and power of the natural world by reading two poems, "The Storm" and "Swift Things Are Beautiful."

Lesson Objectives

- Compare and contrast literary characters and selections.
- Identify theme.
- Identify alliteration.
- Identify and interpret the use of figurative language.
- Identify personification.
- Identify rhythm.
- Recognize use of language to convey mood.

PREPARE

Approximate lesson time is 60 minutes.

Materials

For the Student

Classics for Young Readers, Vol. 6 - pages 306-308

Classics for Young Readers, Vol. 6: An Audio Companion - tracks 16-17

Keywords and Pronunciation

alliteration : the use of words with the same or similar beginning sounds

mood : the emotions or feelings conveyed in a literary work

personification : giving human qualities to a thing or abstraction; for example, "The kettle sang on the hearth," or "After the victory, freedom held its head high in the nation."

rhythm : a regular pattern of sound and beats within a poem

speaker : the imaginary person who speaks the words of a poem, not the poet

theme : the main message that an author wants to communicate to a reader

LEARN
Activity 1: "The Storm" and "Swift Things Are Beautiful" *(Online)*

Activity 2: "The Storm" and "Swift Things Are Beautiful" *(Offline)*

Activity 3: "The Storm" and "Swift Things Are Beautiful" *(Online)*

Activity 4: The Storm *(Online)*

Activity 5: Elizabeth Coatsworth *(Offline)*
Instructions

1. How does the rhythm of the poem change between the first and second stanzas? How does Coatsworth create this change in rhythm with her language? If you need help in answering this question, you may want to listen to the poem again on the *Classics for Young Readers* CD and listen to the way the reader says words differently in each stanza.

   _____

   _____

   _____

   _____

   _____

   _____

2. What do you think is this poem's theme? Use evidence from the text to support your answer.

   _____

   _____

   _____

   _____

Activity 6. Optional: "The Storm" and "Swift Things Are Beautiful" *(Online)*

Student Guide
Lesson 6: "I Wandered Lonely as a Cloud" and "Until I Saw the Sea"

Lesson Objectives

- Compare and contrast literary characters and selections.
- Identify and interpret the use of figurative language.
- Recognize use of language to convey mood.

PREPARE

Approximate lesson time is 60 minutes.

Materials

For the Student

Classics for Young Readers, Vol. 6 - pages 309-311

Classics for Young Readers, Vol. 6: An Audio Companion - tracks 18-19

Reading Notebook

Keywords and Pronunciation

figurative language : language that uses figures of speech such as metaphor, simile, and personification for poetic effect rather than for precise, factual meaning; for example, "Her eyes are like stars" is figurative language, in contrast to the literal use of "stars" in "The stars are shining tonight"

image : a picture evoked from the words in a piece of writing

mood : the emotions or feelings conveyed in a literary work

rhythm : a regular pattern of sound and beats within a poem

speaker : the imaginary person who speaks the words of a poem, not the poet

theme : the main message that an author wants to communicate to a reader

---

LEARN
Activity 1: "I Wandered Lonely as a Cloud" and "Until I Saw the Sea" *(Online)*

Activity 2: "I Wandered Lonely as a Cloud" and "Until I Saw the Sea" *(Offline)*

Activity 3: "I Wandered Lonely as a Cloud" and "Until I Saw the Sea" *(Online)*

Activity 4: Movement and Lilian Moore *(Online)*

Activity 5: The Worth of Wordsworth's Words *(Online)*

Activity 6. Optional: "I Wandered Lonely as a Cloud" and "Until I Saw the Sea" *(Online)*

Student Guide
Lesson 7: "To Everything There Is a Season" and Review

Lesson Objectives

- Compare and contrast literary characters and selections.
- Identify and interpret the use of figurative language.
- Identify characteristics of haiku.
- Identify personification.
- Identify theme.
- Recognize use of language to convey mood.
- Identify alliteration.
- Identify rhyming couplets.
- Identify speaker.

PREPARE

Approximate lesson time is 60 minutes.

Materials

For the Student

Classics for Young Readers, Vol. 6 - page 312

Classics for Young Readers, Vol. 6: An Audio Companion - track 20

Reading Notebook

📖 Reciting Poetry

Keywords and Pronunciation

couplet : A two-line poem that rhymes. For example: The apple on the table is fresh and green. I wanted to eat it without being seen.

mood : the emotions or feelings conveyed in a literary work

personification : giving human qualities to a thing or abstraction; for example, "The kettle sang on the hearth," or "After the victory, freedom held its head high in the nation."

theme : the main message that an author wants to communicate to a reader

LEARN
Activity 1: "To Everything There Is a Season" and Review *(Online)*

Activity 2: "To Everything There Is a Season" and Review *(Offline)*

Activity 3: "To Everything There Is a Season" and Review *(Online)*

Activity 4: "To Everything There Is a Season" *(Online)*

Activity 5: Oral Recitation *(Online)*

Name _____ **Date** _____

Reciting Poetry

A. Listen

Listen to each of the poems again on CD.

How should a poem sound? How do you know how to read it aloud? When should you stop to take a breath? There isn't a single answer to these questions, but poets do offer some clues.

The way the lines break, or where they end, gives you one clue about how to read a poem. And the punctuation can help you, too. Think of the commas as short breaths and the periods as longer beats. Some poets pause lightly at line-breaks, others do not. Reading aloud is also driven by the ups and downs (called cadences) in the language. What syllables are stressed? Which words take longer to say?

Consider which words should be emphasized and which words should not. Would you want to speak loudly and strongly when you recite Robert Frost's "The Pasture"? How do you think that Walter de la Mare's "The Storm" should be recited? Don't forget about the importance of the verbs in Lilian Moore's work. Remember, the reading can influence the experience of the poem, so you should try to make your reading reflect the **mood** and **themes** of the piece.

B. Recite

Try reading a poem aloud, practicing the way you think it should sound. Choose a poem and recite it aloud.

When you have read it through a number of times, try committing a small section or a stanza to memory. Practice reciting that section aloud in preparation for a formal recitation later this semester.

Public Speaking Pointers

- Stand straight and tall.

- Make eye contact with the audience when reciting.

- Keep your hands at your sides unless gesturing to accompany the presentation.

Name   Date

- Speak clearly and loud enough so that everyone can hear you.

- Speak with expression, with feeling. Think ahead about possibly using your hands or facial expressions (a smile, a puzzled look, a frightened look, etc.).

- If you're reading from a book or paper, hold it low enough for the audience to see your face. While reading aloud, occasionally pause and look up.

Student Guide
Lesson 8: Unit Assessment

Lesson Objectives

- Compare and contrast literary characters and selections.
- Demonstrate comprehension of text.
- Identify alliteration.
- Identify and interpret the use of figurative language.
- Identify characteristics of haiku.
- Identify personification.
- Identify rhyming couplets.
- Identify speaker.
- Identify theme.
- Recognize use of language to convey mood.

PREPARE

Approximate lesson time is 60 minutes.

ASSESS

Unit Checkpoint: To Everything There Is a Season, Part 1 (*Online*)

It's time to check what you have learned. Go to the next screen to test your skills.

Unit Checkpoint: To Everything There Is a Season, Part 2 (*Offline*)

It's time to check what you have learned.

1. Gather the Assessment Sheet.
2. Read and follow the instructions to complete the assessment.
3. When you've finished, your Learning Coach will review your work and enter the results online.

Student Guide
Lesson 1: "What's Black and White and Red All Over?"

Lesson Objectives

- Identify defining characteristics of the text.
- Make inferences and draw conclusions.
- Recognize author's purpose and devices used to accomplish it, including author's language, organization, and structure.
- Formulate opinion and personal response.
- Contribute meaningfully to group discussions by being prepared for discussion, drawing on preparation, explaining own ideas, building upon others' comments, and asking questions.

PREPARE

Approximate lesson time is 60 minutes.

Materials

For the Student

MLA Handbook for Writers of Research Papers - MLA (Modern Language Association) Full citation:

MLA Handbook for Writers of Research Papers. 7th ed. New York: MLA, 2009. Print.

Believing Our Ears & Eyes

Reading Notebook

Optional

💻 Guidelines for Peer Discussion

Keywords and Pronunciation

conclusion : the final paragraph of an essay

hook : a surprising or intriguing passage, idea, or image used to grab the reader's attention, usually at the beginning of a work

main idea : the most important point of the paragraph

Oedipus (ED-uh-puhs)

Sphinx (sfingks)

supporting details : the sentences that give information about the main idea or topic sentence

---

LEARN
Activity 1: "What's Black and White and Red All Over?" *(Online)*

Activity 2: "What's Black and White and Red All Over?" *(Online)*

Activity 3: "What's Black and White and Red All Over?" *(Online)*

Activity 4: Riddle Review *(Online)*

Activity 5: Writers Shape Their Craft *(Online)*

Activity 6: Personal Response *(Offline)*

Activity 7: Peer Discussion *(Offline)*

Guidelines for Peer Discussion

Share your thoughts, ideas, questions, and feelings about a text with a peer or others. Listen carefully to what everyone has to say about the text. During your discussion, follow these guidelines.

1. Be prepared to discuss your ideas about the text and to ask and answer questions about what you read. Whenever possible, use examples from the text to support your statements, help others understand your meaning, and justify your answers.

2. Listen carefully and quietly if it's not your turn to speak. Pay attention to what others say so that you can add your ideas. Speak clearly and in complete sentences.

3. Connect and add to the ideas that others have stated using sentences that begin with phrases such as:

    "I understand . . . ."
    "I feel that . . . ."
    "We should also think about how . . . ."
    "That idea relates to . . . ."

4. Respectfully question the opinions of others and politely defend your reasoning if your opinion differs. Use sentences that begin with phrases such as:

    "What do you mean when you say . . .?"
    "Can you give an example of . . .?"
    "I see what you're saying, but what about . . .?"
    "I reacted to that a little differently because . . . ."
    "I disagree with that because . . . ."

5. Draw conclusions about what has already happened in a text and make inferences about what may happen next.

6. Keep the goal(s) of the discussion in mind and respect others. Remember that each member of the group has a valuable contribution to make.

7. Remember that opinions are neither right nor wrong, only different. Remain cordial, thoughtful, and courteous when disagreements or differences of opinion occur.

Student Guide
Lesson 2: "A Thousand Years of Guessing"

You know from the last lesson that riddles are a very old form of humor. The reason we know this is because of a book that is over a thousand years old. The book survives today because monks copied it and preserved it centuries ago. Read on to find out more about the book.

Lesson Objectives

- Make inferences and draw conclusions.
- Identify defining characteristics of the text.
- Recognize author's purpose and devices used to accomplish it, including author's language, organization, and structure.
- Compare and contrast literary characters and selections.
- Formulate opinion and personal response.

PREPARE

Approximate lesson time is 60 minutes.

Materials

For the Student

Believing Our Ears & Eyes

Reading Notebook

LEARN
Activity 1: "A Thousand Years of Guessing" *(Online)*

Activity 2: "A Thousand Years of Guessing" *(Online)*

Activity 3: "A Thousand Years of Guessing" *(Online)*

Activity 4: Compare the Authors *(Online)*

Activity 5: Riddles and Answers *(Offline)*
Instructions
A. Explore the Riddles
What makes riddles puzzling and fun? Examine the riddles on pages 20-21 of *Believing Our Ears and Eyes* and answer these questions.

---

1. Reread each riddle and make a note about any clues you recognize.

   _____

   _____

   _____

   _____

2. Look up any words you do not understand.

3. For riddles #1 and #2, write a one-sentence explanation of the answer. For example, your sentence might begin: The answer to the riddle is *ice* because...

   _____

   _____

   _____

   _____

4. For riddles #3 and #4, choose which of the possible answers you believe is correct and explain why

   _____

   _____

   _____

   _____

B. Write Your Own Riddle

Now you will write your own Who Am I? riddle. Take a look at three more riddles before you begin your own.

1. Give me food, and I will live; give me water, and I will die. What am I?

2. What can run but never walks, has a mouth but never talks, has a head but never weeps, has a bed but never sleeps?

3. Pronounced as one letter,
   And written with three,
   Two letters there are,
   And two only in me.
   I'm double, I'm single,
   I'm black, blue, and gray,
   I'm read from both ends,
   And the same either way.
   What am I?

C. You Try It

You should be creative with your Who Am I? riddle. It can be six lines long, or it can be twenty-six lines long! Here are some things to think about as you write your riddle:

- Select a physical object you encounter every day--for example, a piece of furniture or sports equipment, a favorite souvenir, a snack, a person. Do not choose something so obscure that nobody will be able to guess it.

- Consider the object's physical appearance. What does it look like, feel like, taste like, sound like, smell like?

- What is the object's purpose? What is its relationship to you or to human beings in general?

- Can you associate it with other things? For example, can you think of words with double meanings that can be used to describe your object?

Remember, you want your riddle to be solvable, but you still want it to be a puzzle. Try to play with words and meanings to create a riddle that will have your friends puzzling over it for a while.

If you enjoyed writing the riddle, challenge yourself to write a Who Am I? riddle about something nonphysical-- perhaps an emotion or concept such as love or fear.

Here's an example:

I never was, am always to be,
No one ever saw me, nor ever will,
And yet I am the confidence of all
To live and breathe on this terrestrial ball.
What am I?

Answer: tomorrow

Activity 6. Optional: "A Thousand Years of Guessing" (Online)

Student Guide
Lesson 3: Alice's Adventures in Wonderland: Session 1

Children often enjoy imagining other worlds. You are going to read about a little girl who doesn't imagine a new world. Instead, she falls into one.

Lesson Objectives

- Make inferences and draw conclusions.
- Describe characters based on speech, actions, or interactions with others.
- Identify character traits and motivations.
- Identify defining characteristics of the text.
- Recognize author's purpose and devices used to accomplish it, including author's language, organization, and structure.
- Recognize author's attitude or tone.

PREPARE

Approximate lesson time is 60 minutes.

Materials

For the Student

Reading Notebook

Classics for Young Readers, Vol. 6 - pages 314-330

Classics for Young Readers, Vol. 6: An Audio Companion - track 23

Keywords and Pronunciation

circular reasoning : a logical fallacy in which support for a statement is a restatement of the same idea in different words

parody : a piece of writing that mocks another piece through imitation

LEARN
Activity 1: *Alice's Adventures in Wonderland* - Session 1 *(Online)*

Activity 2: *Alice's Adventures in Wonderland* - Session 1 *(Online)*

Activity 3: *Alice's Adventures in Wonderland* - Session 1 *(Online)*

Activity 4: Language Games *(Online)*

Activity 5: Non-Sense *(Offline)*

Instructions

Lewis Carroll was famous for his wordplay and his nonsense verse. Consider the way the author plays with language and reality.

1. Look up the word *sense* in your dictionary. You will find several definitions. *Sense*, in today's discussion, is the ability to accurately perceive or communicate truths about reality. Now, without looking in your dictionary, write your own definition for the word *nonsense*.

    _____

    _____

    _____

    _____

2. Nonsense is not always meaningless. For example, Carroll uses his poem **parody** "How Doth the Little Crocodile" to create a meaning that is different from the original poem's meaning. By twisting the poem, playing with language, and making the poem ridiculous, he is able to convey his attitude toward moralistic poetry. In some ways, nonsense like Carroll's can help readers make more sense of reality. How might this be true?

    _____

    _____

    _____

    _____

3. Many people have said that Alice's adventures are like a dream or a child's nightmare, where what seems real does not actually follow "real-world" rules. Name some specific ways that today's story has dream-like, or nightmare-like, qualities.

    _____

    _____

    _____

    _____

4. Why might the author have written Wonderland as a nightmarish version of the real world? What might he be trying to suggest by creating a version of the real world instead of a world that is completely different from reality?

    _____

    _____

    _____

    _____

    _____

Activity 6. Optional: *Alice's Adventures in Wonderland* - Session 1 *(Online)*

Student Guide
Lesson 4: Alice's Adventures in Wonderland: Session 2

Alice could use some help. Will she get any from the Caterpillar in today's story?

Lesson Objectives

- Recognize author's purpose and devices used to accomplish it, including author's language, organization, and structure.
- Identify defining characteristics of the text.
- Compare and contrast literary characters and selections.
- Describe characters based on speech, actions, or interactions with others.
- Identify character traits and motivations.
- Recognize author's attitude or tone.

PREPARE

Approximate lesson time is 60 minutes.

Materials

For the Student

Classics for Young Readers, Vol. 6 - pages 330-337

🖳 A Poem and Its Parody

🖳 Comparing Poems

Reading Notebook

Keywords and Pronunciation

dialogue : a conversation between characters

figurative language : language that uses figures of speech such as metaphor, simile, and personification for poetic effect rather than for precise, factual meaning; for example, "Her eyes are like stars" is figurative language, in contrast to the literal use of "stars" in "The stars are shining tonight"

parody : a piece of writing that mocks another piece through imitation

theme : the main message that an author wants to communicate to a reader

tone : the writer's attitude toward the topic or subject

LEARN
Activity 1: *Alice's Adventures in Wonderland* - Session 2 *(Online)*

Activity 2: *Alice's Adventures in Wonderland* - Session 2 *(Online)*

Activity 3: *Alice's Adventures in Wonderland* - Session 2 *(Online)*

Activity 4: A Confusing Conversation *(Online)*

Activity 5: "Father William" *(Online)*

Activity 6: What Do the Pictures Say? *(Offline)*
Instructions

1. Look at the pictures of Alice on pages 320-321. Does Alice look like a typical child? Why or why not?

   _____

   _____

   _____

2. Look at Alice on page 324, after she has taken a bit of the cake that says "EAT ME." How would you describe the picture?

   _____

   _____

   _____

3. Now peek ahead to the other illustrations in the chapters that follow. (The last illustration is on page 346.) Can you make a general statement about the illustrations?

   _____

   _____

   _____

   _____

   _____

Activity 7: More Illustrations *(Online)*

Name   Date

A Poem and Its Parody

"The Old Man's Complaints and How He Gained Them" by Robert Southey (1774-1843)

You are old, Father William, the young man cried,
The few locks which are left you are grey;
You are hale, Father William, a hearty old man,
Now tell me the reason I pray.

In the days of my youth, Father William replied,
I remember'd that youth would fly fast,
Abused not my health and my vigour at first
That I never might need them at last.

You are old, Father William, the young man cried,
And pleasures with youth pass away,
And yet you lament not the days that are gone,
Now tell me the reason I pray.

In the days of my youth, Father William replied,
I remember'd that youth could not last;
I thought of the future whatever I did,
That I never might grieve for the past.

You are old, Father William, the young man cried,
And life must be hastening away;
You are chearful, and love to converse upon death!
Now tell me the reason I pray.

I am chearful, young man, Father William replied,
Let the cause thy attention engage;
In the days of my youth I remember'd my God!
And He hath not forgotten my age.

"Father William" by Lewis Carroll

"You are old, Father William," the young man said,
"And your hair has become very white;
And yet you incessantly stand on your head—
Do you think, at your age, it is right?"

"In my youth," Father William replied to his son,
"I feared it might injure the brain;
But, now that I'm perfectly sure I have none,
Why, I do it again and again."

"You are old," said the youth, "as I mentioned before,
And have grown most uncommonly fat;
Yet you turned a back-somersault in at the door—
Pray, what is the reason of that?"

"In my youth," said the sage, as he shook his gray locks,
"I kept all my limbs very supple
By the use of this ointment —one shilling the box—
Allow me to sell you a couple."

"You are old," said the youth, "and your jaws are too weak
For anything tougher than suet;
Yet you finished the goose, with the bones and the beak—
Pray, how did you manage to do it?"

"In my youth," said his father, "I took to the law,
And argued each case with my wife;
And the muscular strength, which it gave to my jaw
Has lasted the rest of my life."

"You are old," said the youth; "one would hardly suppose
That your eye was as steady as ever;
Yet you balanced an eel on the end of your nose—
What made you so awfully clever?"

"I have answered three questions, and that is enough,"
Said his father; "don't give yourself airs!
Do you think I can listen all day to such stuff?
Be off, or I'll kick you downstairs!"

Name _____ Date _____

Comparing Poems

Compare and contrast Robert Southey's original poem "The Old Man's Complaints and How He Gained Them" and Carroll's parody.

1. What did Southey's Father William do in his youth?

   _____

   _____

   _____

   _____

2. How would you describe Southey's Father William?

   _____

   _____

   _____

   _____

3. What did Carroll's Father William do in his youth?

   _____

   _____

   _____

   _____

   _____

4. How would you describe Carroll's Father William?

   _____

   _____

   _____

   _____

   _____

5. Look at the illustrations on pages 333-335. What attitude do the illustrations portray?

   _____

   _____

   _____

   _____

Name _____   Date _____

6. Write another question and answer for either Southey's version or Carroll's version of "Father William."

_____

_____

_____

_____

_____

_____

_____

_____

_____

_____

Student Guide
Lesson 5: Alice's Adventures in Wonderland: Session 3

Will Alice continue eating this and that to make her way through Wonderland?

Lesson Objectives

- Compare and contrast literary characters and selections.
- Describe characters based on speech, actions, or interactions with others.
- Identify character traits and motivations.
- Recognize author's purpose and devices used to accomplish it, including author's language, organization, and structure.

PREPARE

Approximate lesson time is 60 minutes.

Materials

For the Student

Classics for Young Readers, Vol. 6 - pages 337-341

Reading Notebook

LEARN
Activity 1: *Alice's Adventures in Wonderland* - Session 3 *(Online)*

Activity 2: *Alice's Adventures in Wonderland* - Session 3 *(Online)*

Activity 3: Making Meaning *(Online)*

Activity 4: Not All Nonsense *(Offline)*
Instructions
Think about the following statements of the Chesire Cat. Are they pure nonsense? Why or why not?

1. What truth about the real world of human beings is contained in the Cat's statement, "Oh, you can't help that...we're all mad here. I'm mad. You're mad"?

   _____

   _____

   _____

   _____

---

2. Alice asks the Cat which way she ought to go, and the Cat responds: "That depends a good deal on where you want to get to." What is the sense behind this nonsense?

_____

_____

_____

_____

3. Find another statement from a Wonderland character that may be more than nonsense and explain your selection.

_____

_____

_____

_____

Student Guide
Lesson 6: Alice's Adventures in Wonderland: Session 4

Lesson Objectives

- Make inferences and draw conclusions.
- Recognize author's purpose and devices used to accomplish it, including author's language, organization, and structure.
- Describe characters based on speech, actions, or interactions with others.
- Formulate opinion and personal response.
- Identify character traits and motivations.
- Identify defining characteristics of the text.

PREPARE

Approximate lesson time is 60 minutes.

Materials

> For the Student
>> Classics for Young Readers, Vol. 6 - pages 342-351
>> Reading Notebook

Keywords and Pronunciation

climax : the point of highest action in a story; the turning point

personification : giving human qualities to a thing or abstraction; for example, "The kettle sang on the hearth," or "After the victory, freedom held its head high in the nation."

LEARN
Activity 1: *Alice's Adventures in Wonderland* - Session 4 *(Online)*

Activity 2: *Alice's Adventures in Wonderland* - Session 4 *(Online)*

Activity 3: *Alice's Adventures in Wonderland* - Session 4 *(Online)*

Activity 4: Ridiculous Reality *(Online)*

Activity 5: Who or What Is Time? *(Online)*

Student Guide
Lesson 7: "The Walrus and the Carpenter"

You have seen that Lewis Carroll enjoyed writing parodies of popular poems. He also enjoyed writing his own poems, one of which you will read in today's lesson.

Lesson Objectives

- Formulate opinion and personal response.
- Identify characteristics of narrative poetry.
- Identify defining characteristics of the text.
- Make inferences and draw conclusions.
- Compare and contrast literary characters and selections.
- Describe characters based on speech, actions, or interactions with others.
- Identify character traits and motivations.
- Recognize author's attitude or tone.
- Identify conflict and resolution.

PREPARE

Approximate lesson time is 60 minutes.

Materials

For the Student

Classics for Young Readers, Vol. 6 - pages 352-357

Classics for Young Readers, Vol. 6: An Audio Companion - track 24

Optional

📖 "Jabberwocky" by Lewis Carroll

Keywords and Pronunciation

conflict : a clash or struggle between people, ideas, or feelings; characters can have a conflict within themselves, with another character, with society, or with nature

narrative poem : a poem that tells a story

resolution : the solution or working out of a literary conflict

tone : the writer's attitude toward the topic or subject

LEARN
Activity 1: "The Walrus and the Carpenter" (Online)

Activity 2: "The Walrus and the Carpenter" (Online)

Activity 3: "The Walrus and the Carpenter" *(Online)*

Activity 4: Fun with Words *(Online)*

Activity 5: Think About It *(Offline)*
Instructions

1. Look at the illustration in your book on page 354. Describe the appearance of the Walrus and the Carpenter. Does the illustration portray the **tone** of the poem? Why or why not? Use evidence from the text to support your answer.

   _____

   _____

   _____

   _____

   _____

   _____

2. This poem is full of humorous nonsense that makes readers laugh. Does it evoke any other feelings? Why or why not? Use evidence from the text to support your answer.

   _____

   _____

   _____

   _____

   _____

   _____

Activity 6. Optional: "The Walrus and the Carpenter" *(Online)*

Name_____   Date_____

"Jabberwocky" by Lewis Carroll

"Twas brilling, and the slithy toves
        Did gyre and gimble in the wabe:
All mimsy were the borogoves,
            And the mome raths outgrabe.

"Beware the Jabberwock, my son!
        The jaws that bite, the claws that catch!
Beware the Jubjub bird, and shun
            The frumious Bandersnatch!"

He took his vorpal sword in hand:
        Long time the manxome foe he sought —
So rested he by the Tumtum tree,
            And stood awhile in thought.

And, as in uffish thought he stood,
        The Jabberwock, with eyes of flame,
Came Wiffling through the tulgey wood,
            And burbled as it came!

One, two! One, two! And through and through
        The vorpal blade went snicker-snack!
He left it dead, and with its head
            He went galumphing back.

"And hast thou slain the Jabberwock?
        Come to my arms, my beamish boy!
O frabjous day! Callooh! Callay!"
            He chortled in his joy.

'Twas brilling, and the slithy toves
        Did gyre and gimble in the wabe:
All mimsy were the borogoves,
            And the mome raths outgrabe.

Student Guide
Lesson 8: "A Selection of Limericks"

Lewis Carroll is not alone in his love of playful language. In today's lesson, you will read some of the clever poems of another Victorian, Edward Lear.

Lesson Objectives

- Make inferences and draw conclusions.
- Recognize author's purpose and devices used to accomplish it, including author's language, organization, and structure.
- Identify meter.
- Recognize poetic devices including rhyme, syllabification, and meter.
- Identify character traits and motivations.
- Identify defining characteristics of the text.
- Recognize author's attitude or tone.
- Identify the characteristics of a limerick.
- Identify the characteristics of a nonsense poem.

PREPARE

Approximate lesson time is 60 minutes.

Materials

For the Student

Classics for Young Readers, Vol. 6 - pages 358-359

Classics for Young Readers, Vol. 6: An Audio Companion - track 21

Reading Notebook

Keywords and Pronunciation

meter : the arrangement of words in poetry based on rhythm, accents, and the number of syllables in a line

nonce : a word that is created for an instance or occasion

portmanteau : a word that is made by taking two or more words that are descriptive and combining them into a new word

rhyme scheme : the pattern of rhymes made by the final words or sounds in the lines of a poem, typically designated by a different letter of the alphabet to represent each rhyme

rhyming couplet : two consecutive lines of poetry that rhyme

tone : the writer's attitude toward the topic or subject

LEARN
Activity 1: "A Selection of Limericks" (Online)

Activity 2: "A Selection of Limericks" (Online)

Activity 3: "A Selection of Limericks" *(Online)*

Activity 4: Elements of a Limerick *(Online)*

Activity 5: Write Your Own Limerick *(Offline)*

Instructions

You are going to write your own limerick. Remember that limericks are essentially nonsense, so you need not worry about creating imagery or a theme.

Begin by playing with words. Think of a funny word you like or an idea you want to make funny. Brainstorm rhyming words. Use the limerick structure to write your limerick.

If you don't have any ideas, you might start with a line like this:

There once was a _____ from _____.

OR

I once met a _____ from _____.

Remember the following requirements:

Number of lines: 5
Syllables per line: 8, 8, 5, 5, 8
Meter: 3, 3, 2, 2, 3
Rhyme scheme: AABBA

_____

_____

_____

_____

_____

_____

_____

_____

Activity 6. Optional: "A Selection of Limericks" *(Online)*

Student Guide
Lesson 9: A Little Nash Menagerie

Lesson Objectives

- Recognize author's purpose and devices used to accomplish it, including author's language, organization, and structure.
- Compare and contrast literary characters and selections.
- Formulate opinion and personal response.
- Identify defining characteristics of the text.
- Identify rhythm and rhyme scheme.
- Recognize author's attitude or tone.

PREPARE

Approximate lesson time is 60 minutes.

Materials

For the Student

Classics for Young Readers, Vol. 6 - pages 360-361

Classics for Young Readers, Vol. 6: An Audio Companion - track 22

Reading Notebook

Keywords and Pronunciation

meter : the arrangement of words in poetry based on rhythm, accents, and the number of syllables in a line

nonce : a word that is created for an instance or occasion

rhyme scheme : the pattern of rhymes made by the final words or sounds in the lines of a poem, typically designated by a different letter of the alphabet to represent each rhyme

rhythm : a regular pattern of sound and beats within a poem

LEARN
Activity 1: "A Little Nash Menagerie" *(Online)*

Activity 2: "A Little Nash Menagerie" *(Online)*

Activity 3: "A Little Nash Menagerie" *(Online)*

Activity 4: Rule-Breaking Poetry *(Online)*

Activity 5: Humorous Writers *(Online)*

Activity 6. Optional: "A Little Nash Menagerie" *(Online)*

Student Guide
Lesson 10: Unit Assessment

Lesson Objectives

- Compare and contrast literary characters and selections.
- Describe characters based on speech, actions, or interactions with others.
- Identify character traits and motivations.
- Identify defining characteristics of the text.
- Identify the characteristics of a limerick.
- Identify the characteristics of a nonsense poem.
- Make inferences and draw conclusions.
- Recognize author's attitude or tone.
- Recognize author's purpose and devices used to accomplish it, including author's language, organization, and structure.
- Formulate opinion and personal response.
- Identify theme.
- Make inferences and draw conclusions.

PREPARE

Approximate lesson time is 60 minutes.

ASSESS

Unit Checkpoint: Stuff and Nonsense, Part 1 (*Online*)

It's time to check what you have learned. Go to the next screen to test your skills.

Unit Checkpoint: Stuff and Nonsense, Part 2 (*Offline*)

It's time to check what you have learned.

1. Gather the Assessment Sheet.
2. Read and follow the instructions to complete the assessment.
3. When you've finished, your Learning Coach will review your work and enter the results online.

Student Guide
Lesson 1: Twelfth Night: Act I

After her ship is wrecked during a storm, a young woman must find a way to survive in an unfamiliar country.

Lesson Objectives

- Demonstrate knowledge of authors, characters, and events of historically or culturally significant works of literature.
- Identify defining characteristics of drama.
- Compare and contrast text with visual or aural presentation.
- Describe characters based on speech, actions, or interactions with others.
- Identify character traits and motivations.
- Identify theme.
- Contribute meaningfully to group discussions by being prepared for discussion, drawing on preparation, explaining own ideas, building upon others' comments, and asking questions.

PREPARE

Approximate lesson time is 60 minutes.

Materials

For the Student

MLA Handbook for Writers of Research Papers - MLA(Modern Language Association) Full citation:

MLA Handbook for Writers of Research Papers.7th ed. New York: MLA, 2009. Print.

Classics for Young Readers, Vol. 6: An Audio Companion - Track 28

Shakespeare for Young People: Twelfth Night - pages 12-25

Optional

📇 Glossary

📇 Guidelines for Peer Discussion

Keywords and Pronunciation

conflict : a clash or struggle between people, ideas, or feelings; characters can have a conflict within themselves, with another character, with society, or with nature

protagonist (proh-TAG-uh-nist) : the main character; the character around whom the action of the plot centers

LEARN
Activity 1: *Twelfth Night* - Act I *(Online)*

Activity 2: *Twelfth Night* - Act I *(Offline)*
Instructions
<u>Vocabulary for Act I:</u>

strain: a short tune or musical passage

fall: chords that end a piece of music

hence: from now

season: to keep something fresh; to mark a period of time with a certain set of characteristics

Elysium: in Greek mythology, where honored or good people go after they die

Arion on the dolphin's back: from a Greek myth, a young musician who is forced to leap out of a ship, but is saved from drowning by a dolphin that is charmed by his music

hold acquaintance: stay afloat; not be swallowed up

abjured: avoided

allow me very worth his service: to be very useful to someone

plague: means both irritation and disastrous evil

By my troth: epithet meaning "My word!"

takes great exceptions: strongly objects

ducats: gold coins used in Europe many years ago

shrew: a woman who frequently scolds others

caper: a playful leap or dance

clamorous: noisy

prosper well: be successful

barful strife: a task that can only be completed by overcoming many obstacles

madonna: an Italian word used to address a woman politely; means "my lady"

slander: a false statement that damages someone's reputation

sot: a person who is often drunk

blent: blended

cantons: love songs

reverberate: that which echoes

soft: wait, or "Wait a minute!"

peevish: stubborn and ill-tempered

hie thee: hurry

Activity 3: *Twelfth Night* - Act I *(Online)*

Activity 4: The Folly of *Twelfth Night* *(Online)*

Activity 5: Love in *Twelfth Night* *(Online)*

Activity 6. Optional: *Twelfth Night* - Act I *(Online)*

Activity 7: Peer Discussion *(Offline)*

Glossary

Twelfth Night

Here is a list of words that you will find in the reading for this unit.

Act I
strain: a short tune or musical passage
fall: chords that end a piece of music
hence: from now
season: to keep something fresh; to mark a period of time with a certain set of characteristics
Elysium: in Greek mythology, where honored or good people go after they die
Arion on the dolphin's back: from a Greek myth, a young musician who is forced to leap out of a ship, but is saved from drowning by a dolphin that is charmed by his music
hold acquaintance: stay afloat; not be swallowed up
abjured: avoided
allow me very worth his service: to be very useful to someone
plague: means both irritation and disastrous evil
By my troth: epithet meaning "My word!"
takes great exceptions: strongly objects
ducats: gold coins used in Europe many years ago
shrew: a woman who frequently scolds others
caper: a playful leap or dance
clamorous: noisy
prosper well: be successful
barful strife: a task that can only be completed by overcoming many obstacles
madonna: an Italian word used to address a woman politely; means "my lady"
slander: a false statement that damages someone's reputation
sot: a person who is often drunk
blent: blended
cantons: love songs
reverberate: that which echoes
soft: wait, or "Wait a minute!"
peevish: stubborn and ill-tempered
hie thee: hurry

Act II
accounted: considered
outside: disguise
betimes: in good time; early
dulcet: pleasing to listen to; melodious
stoup: cup
uncivil: rude
epistles: formal letters
contemplative: a person thinking hard

Glossary

sport royal: a clever trick
yew: an evergreen tree
let all the rest give place: it is time for everyone else to go
sovereign: the leader or person in charge
concealment: the state of hiding something
damask: a luxurious fabric with designs woven on it
Signior: an Italian word used to respectfully address a man, means "mister"
Fortune: destiny, fate
perchance: perhaps
scab: a person who merits contempt
commended: praised
wished to see thee ever cross-gartered: wanted to see you always wearing crossed-garters
garters: bands worn to hold up a person's stockings or socks
device: trick

Act III
Westward-ho!: I'm leaving
sought to have: purposely wanted to find something
adieu: a French word that means good-bye
marry: a word used to emphasize what is being said
write it in a martial hand: to write as if one was a great warrior, or as if preparing for war
curst: as if cursing something
the new map with the augmentation of the Indies: a map printed during Shakespeare's time that had many lines on it
haply: perhaps
tainted in his wits: crazy; out of his mind
obstruction: something that blocks a way or passage
waylay: to ambush or attack
beseech: to beg
remedy: a cure; a way to fix something
necessity: a need

Act IV
hold: stop
curate: a clergyman
knavery: dishonesty, cruel mischief

Act V
dissembling: lying
durance: being held by force
semblance: outward appearance
notorious: well-known in an unfavorable way
recompense: something given in return
estate: one's social rank and physical inheritance

Guidelines for Peer Discussion

Share your thoughts, ideas, questions, and feelings about a text with a peer or others. Listen carefully to what everyone has to say about the text. During your discussion, follow these guidelines.

1. Be prepared to discuss your ideas about the text and to ask and answer questions about what you read. Whenever possible, use examples from the text to support your statements, help others understand your meaning, and justify your answers.

2. Listen carefully and quietly if it's not your turn to speak. Pay attention to what others say so that you can add your ideas. Speak clearly and in complete sentences.

3. Connect and add to the ideas that others have stated using sentences that begin with phrases such as:

   "I understand . . . ."
   "I feel that . . . ."
   "We should also think about how . . . ."
   "That idea relates to . . . ."

4. Respectfully question the opinions of others and politely defend your reasoning if your opinion differs. Use sentences that begin with phrases such as:

   "What do you mean when you say . . .?"
   "Can you give an example of . . .?"
   "I see what you're saying, but what about . . .?"
   "I reacted to that a little differently because . . . ."
   "I disagree with that because . . . ."

5. Draw conclusions about what has already happened in a text and make inferences about what may happen next.

6. Keep the goal(s) of the discussion in mind and respect others. Remember that each member of the group has a valuable contribution to make.

7. Remember that opinions are neither right nor wrong, only different. Remain cordial, thoughtful, and courteous when disagreements or differences of opinion occur.

Student Guide
Lesson 2: Twelfth Night: Act II

Will the love triangle become a square when another suitor attempts to win Olivia's hand?

Lesson Objectives

- Demonstrate knowledge of authors, characters, and events of historically or culturally significant works of literature.
- Recognize the effect of setting or culture on a literary work.
- Describe characters based on speech, actions, or interactions with others.
- Identify character traits and motivations.
- Identify and interpret the use of subplots.
- Identify theme.

PREPARE

Approximate lesson time is 60 minutes.

Materials

For the Student

Shakespeare for Young People: Twelfth Night - pages 26-40

Reading Notebook

Keywords and Pronunciation

plot : what happens in a story; the sequence of events

conflict : a clash or struggle between people, ideas, or feelings; characters can have a conflict within themselves, with another character, with society, or with nature

meter : the arrangement of words in poetry based on rhythm, accents, and the number of syllables in a line

resolution : the solution or working out of a literary conflict

rhythm : a regular pattern of sound and beats within a poem

subplot : a story line or plot that is secondary to the main plot

theme : the main message that an author wants to communicate to a reader

LEARN
Activity 1: *Twelfth Night* - Act II *(Online)*

Activity 2: *Twelfth Night* - Act II *(Offline)*

Instructions

Vocabulary for Act II:

accounted: considered

outside: disguise

betimes: in good time; early

dulcet: pleasing to listen to; melodious

stoup: cup

uncivil: rude

epistles: formal letters

contemplative: a person thinking hard

sport royal: a clever trick

yew: an evergreen tree

let all the rest give place: it is time for everyone else to go

sovereign: the leader or person in charge

concealment: the state of hiding something

damask: a luxurious fabric with designs woven on it

Signior: an Italian word used to respectfully address a man, means "mister"

fortune: destiny, fate

perchance: perhaps

scab: a person who merits contempt

commended: praised

wished to see thee ever cross-gartered: wanted to see you always wearing crossed-garters

garters: bands worn to hold up a person's stockings or socks

device: trick

Activity 3: *Twelfth Night* - Act II *(Online)*

Activity 4: Main Plot, Conflict, and Subplot *(Online)*

Activity 5: Is This True Love? *(Online)*

Activity 6. Optional: *Twelfth Night* - Act II *(Online)*

Student Guide
Lesson 3: Twelfth Night: Act III

More characters arrive on the scene, adding to the confusion. Will this knot become too tangled for even Time to untie?

Lesson Objectives

- Demonstrate knowledge of authors, characters, and events of historically or culturally significant works of literature.
- Identify and interpret the use of subplots.
- Identify conflict and resolution.
- Identify defining characteristics of drama.
- Recognize use of language to convey mood.

PREPARE

Approximate lesson time is 60 minutes.

Materials

For the Student

Shakespeare for Young People: Twelfth Night - pages 41-51

Keywords and Pronunciation

dialogue : a conversation between characters

mood : the emotions or feelings conveyed in a literary work

subplot : a story line or plot that is secondary to the main plot

LEARN
Activity 1: *Twelfth Night* - Act III *(Online)*

Activity 2: *Twelfth Night* - Act III *(Offline)*
Instructions
Vocabulary for Act III

Westward-ho!: I'm leaving

sought to have: purposely wanted to find something

adieu: a French word that means good-bye

marry: a word used to emphasize what is being said

write it in a martial hand: to write as if one was a great warrior, or as if preparing for war

curst: as if cursing something

the new map with the augmentation of the Indies: a map printed during Shakespeare's time that had many lines on it

haply: perhaps

tainted in her wits: crazy; out of her mind

obstruction: something that blocks a way or passage

waylay: to ambush or attack

beseech: to beg

remedy: a cure; a way to fix something

necessity: a need

Activity 3: *Twelfth Night* - Act III *(Online)*

Activity 4: Is This True Love? *(Online)*

Activity 5: Bringing the Dream to Life *(Online)*

Activity 6. Optional: *Twelfth Night* - Act III *(Online)*

Student Guide
Lesson 4: All the World's a Stage

Enter Shakespeare's theater, listen to a performance of a scene from *Twelfth Night,* and don your thespian's garb to act out a passage from the play yourself!

Lesson Objectives

- Demonstrate knowledge of authors, characters, and events of historically or culturally significant works of literature.
- Describe characters based on speech, actions, or interactions with others.
- Identify character traits and motivations.
- Identify defining characteristics of drama.
- Identify theme.

PREPARE

Approximate lesson time is 60 minutes.

Materials

For the Student

📖 Selections from Twelfth Night: Act 1, Scene 5

Classics for Young Readers, Vol. 6: An Audio Companion - track 28

Optional

📖 To Coin a Phrase

Keywords and Pronunciation

figurative language : language that uses figures of speech such as metaphor, simile, and personification for poetic effect rather than for precise, factual meaning; for example, "Her eyes are like stars" is figurative language, in contrast to the literal use of "stars" in "The stars are shining tonight"

image : a picture evoked from the words in a piece of writing

mood : the emotions or feelings conveyed in a literary work

tone : the writer's attitude toward the topic or subject

LEARN
Activity 1: All the World's a Stage *(Online)*

Activity 2: *Twelfth Night* *(Offline)*

Activity 3: Emphasis, Speed, and Tone *(Online)*

Activity 4: Language in Action *(Online)*

Activity 5: Read and Recite *(Offline)*
Instructions
Choose one of the following passages to recite:

1. Act I, Duke Orsino: If music be the food of love, play on! That strain again! It had a dying fall. O, it came o'er my ear like the sweet sound that breathes upon a bank of violets, stealing and giving odour! How now? What news from her?

2. Act I, Viola: Make me a willow cabin at your gate, and call upon my soul within the house. Write loyal cantons of condemned love and sing them loud even in the dead of night. Holla your name to the reverberate hills, and make the babbling gossip of the air cry out, "Olivia!" O, you should not rest between the elements of air and earth, but you should pity me!

3. Act II, Viola: What means this lady? Fortune forbid, my outside have not charmed her! She loves me, sure! Poor lady, she were better love a dream! My master loves her dearly, and I, poor monster, fond as much on him. And she, mistaken, seems to dote on me. What will become of this? O Time, thou must untangle this, not I. It is to hard a knot for me to untie!

4. Act II, Malvolio: "M, O, A, I, doth sway my life!" Nay, but first, let me see, let me see, let me see! "I may command where I adore." Why, she may command me. I serve her. She is my lady! And the end--if I could make that resemble something in me...Softly! M, O, A, I ..."M"--Malvolio! Why, that begins my name! ...Soft! Here follows prose. "In my stars, I am above thee, but be not afraid of greatness. Some are born great, some achieve greatness, and some have greatness thrust upon 'em!"

Mark in the passage where you will use emphasis, speed, and tone to add expression to your reading. You may memorize the passage or read it from the page, but do your best to speak the words as you think the character would say them.

If you want to, you may dress in costume, use props, and act out more of the play.

Activity 6. Optional: All the World's a Stage *(Online)*

Name _____

Date _____

Selections from *Twelfth Night*
Track 31, Act 1, Scene 5

VIOLA: My lord and master loves you: O, such love
  Could be but **recompensed**, though you were
    crown'd
  The **nonpareil** of beauty!

OLIVIA: How does he love me?

VIOLA: With adorations, fertile tears,
  With groans that thunder love, with sighs of fire.

OLIVIA: Your lord does know my mind; I cannot love him:
  Yet I suppose him virtuous, know him noble,
  Of great estate, of fresh and stainless youth;
  In voices **well divulged,** free, learn'd and valiant;
  And in dimension and the shape of nature
  A gracious person: but yet I cannot love him;
  He might have took his answer long ago.

VIOLA: If I did love you in my master's flame,
  With such a suffering, such a deadly life,
  In your **denial** I would find no sense;
  I would not understand it.

OLIVIA: Why, what would you?

VIOLA: Write loyal cantons of **contemned** love
  And sing them loud even in the dead of night;
  Halloo your name to the reverberate hills
  And make the babbling gossip of the air
  Cry out 'Olivia!' O, You should not rest
  Between the elements of air and earth,
  But you should pity me!

OLIVIA: You might do much.
  What is your parentage?

VIOLA: Above my fortunes, yet my state is well:
  I am a gentleman.

OLIVIA: Get you to your lord;
  I cannot love him: let him send no more;
  Unless, perchance, you come to me again,
  To tell me how he takes it. Fare you well:
  I thank you for your pains: spend this for me.

VIOLA: I am no **fee'd** post, lady; keep your purse:
  My master, not myself, lacks recompense.
  Love make his heart of flint that you shall love;
  And let your **fervor**, like my master's, be
  Placed in contempt! Farewell, fair cruelty.

VIOLA: Duke Orsino loves you. Even if you were the most beautiful woman on earth, you should still return his love.

OLIVIA: Describe Orsino's love to me.

VIOLA: Duke Orsino speaks adoringly of you, and cries, sighs, and groans over his love.

OLIVIA: Duke Orsino knows that I will not love anyone. I know he is a good man: noble, of high rank, youthful, well thought of, educated, brave, handsome, and generous. But I cannot love him. Orsino should have accepted this answer a long time ago.

VIOLA: If I loved you as much as Duke Orsino loves you, I wouldn't accept your answer nor would I find it sensible.

OLIVIA: What would you do?

VIOLA: I would write songs about doomed love and sing them all night long. I would call your name so that the hills would echo it and make the air and wind cry out "Olivia." You are too good for this world, but you should pity me.

OLIVIA: That could work. What family are you from?

VIOLA: My family is better than my current position. I am a gentleman.

OLIVIA: Go back to the Duke. I cannot love him, so tell him to stop sending things--unless you return to tell me how he reacted to the news. Good-bye and thank you. Here is some money for your trouble.

VIOLA: I am not a paid servant, m'am. Keep your money. My master should be paid back for his trouble, not me. I hope that when you fall in love, the man's heart will be as hard as yours is now, and your loving feelings, too, will be rejected. Good-bye, beautiful, cruel Olivia!

Name   Date

[Exit]

OLIVIA: 'What is your parentage?'
    'Above my fortunes, yet my state is well:
    I am a gentleman.' I'll be sworn thou art;
    Thy tongue, thy face, thy limbs, actions and spirit,
    Do give thee **five-fold blazon**: not too fast:
    soft, soft!
    Unless the master were the man. How now!
    Even so quickly may one catch the plague?
    Methinks I feel this youth's perfections
    With an invisible and **subtle** stealth
    To creep in at mine eyes. Well, let it be.
    What ho, Malvolio!

[Re-enter MALVOLIO]

MALVOLIO: Here, madam, at your service.

OLIVIA: Run after that same peevish messenger,
    The county's man: he left this ring behind him,
    Would I or not: tell him I'll none of it.
    Desire him not to flatter with his lord,
    Nor hold him up with hopes; I am not for him:
    If that the youth will come this way to-morrow,
    I'll give him reasons for't: hie thee, Malvolio.

MALVOLIO: Madam, I will.

[Exit]

OLIVIA: I do I know not what, and fear to find
    Mine eye too great a flatterer for my mind.
    Fate, show thy force: ourselves we do not owe;
    What is **decreed** must be, and be this so.

[Exit]

OLIVIA: "What family are you from?" "My family is better than my current position. I am a gentleman." I'm sure you are! The way you speak, look, and act clearly shows that you are of nobility. But wait! I wish Duke Orsino was Cesario's servant, and Cesario the master! How is this possible? Can a person fall in love as quickly as she can catch the plague? I think that this boy's charms are quietly working on me. Well, so be it. Malvolio, come here!

[Re-enter MALVOLIO]

MALVOLIO: Here I am. I am at your service.

OLIVIA: Go after Duke Orsino's rude messenger. He left this ring, even though I did not want it. Tell him not to give Orsino good news or raise his hopes, because I will not have him. But if the young man comes tomorrow, I will tell him why I cannot love the Duke. Hurry, Malvolio.

MALVOLIO: I will, my lady.

[Exit]

OLIVIA: I don't know what I'm doing. I am afraid that Cesario is not as wonderful as he appears to be. It's up to Fate now. It's out of my hands and whatever is supposed to be will be.

Vocabulary:

recompensed: returned
nonpareil: that which has no equal
well-divulged: well-known by the people
denial: refusal
contemned: doomed
halloo: to hail loudly; to cry out
fee'd: paid
fervor: strong feelings
five-fold blazon: the marks of nobility
subtle: skillful
decreed: ordered

Name _____ Date _____

To Coin a Phrase

A. Directions
Read these words and expressions that William Shakespeare invented. Discuss their meanings. Choose two, write them below, and give a definition for each. Use each one in a sentence.

budge an inch	dead as a doornail	tower of strength
green-eyed with jealousy	gloomy	fair play
tongue-tied	eyesore	the long and short of it
knit your brow	a laughingstock	excellent
it's Greek to me	lovely	lie low
hoodwinked	slept not one wink	suspect foul play
in a pickle	it's high time	without rhyme or reason

B. Example
Word/Expression: tower of strength
Meaning: a person who is strong during a time of crisis
Sentence: Chris was a tower of strength when the power went out; he calmed everyone's fears, gave out candles and flashlights, and made sure everyone had something for supper.

1. Word/Expression:
   Meaning: _____

   _____

   Sentence: _____

   _____

2. Word/Expression:
   Meaning: _____

   _____

   Sentence: _____

   _____

C. Challenge
Use as many words and phrases as you can in a paragraph or short story. If you want to, you may also use other Shakespearean words and phrases you have learned in this unit.

_____

_____

_____

_____

_____

124

Student Guide
Lesson 5: Twelfth Night: Act IV

In Act IV, the members of Olivia's household meet Viola's twin brother, Sebastian. Do you think his presence will add to their confusion or resolve it?

Lesson Objectives

- Demonstrate knowledge of authors, characters, and events of historically or culturally significant works of literature.
- Describe characters based on speech, actions, or interactions with others.
- Identify character traits and motivations.
- Identify theme.
- Identify defining characteristics of drama.

PREPARE

Approximate lesson time is 60 minutes.

Materials

For the Student

Shakespeare for Young People: Twelfth Night - pages 52-55

Keywords and Pronunciation

sonnet : a 14-line poem, usually in iambic pentameter (a specific meter) that is usually rhymed; the two most familiar kinds of sonnets are the Italian (or Petrarchan) and the English (or Shakespearean)

subplot : a story line or plot that is secondary to the main plot

---

LEARN
Activity 1: *Twelfth Night* - Act IV *(Online)*

Activity 2: *Twelfth Night* - Act IV *(Offline)*

Instructions

Vocabulary for Act IV:

hold: stop

curate: a clergyman

knavery: dishonesty, cruel mischief

Activity 3: *Twelfth Night* - Act IV *(Online)*

Activity 4: The Folly of *Twelfth Night* *(Online)*

Activity 5: Fools and Foolishness *(Online)*

Activity 6. Optional: *Twelfth Night* - Act IV *(Online)*

Student Guide
Lesson 6: Twelfth Night: Act V

Finally, all of the characters come face to face at Duke Orsino's house. How will they sort out this confusion? Can this comedy end happily?

Lesson Objectives

- Demonstrate knowledge of authors, characters, and events of historically or culturally significant works of literature.
- Describe characters based on speech, actions, or interactions with others.
- Identify character traits and motivations.
- Identify defining characteristics of drama.
- Identify theme.

PREPARE

Approximate lesson time is 60 minutes.

Materials

For the Student

Shakespeare for Young People: Twelfth Night - pages 56-62

Keywords and Pronunciation

plot : what happens in a story; the sequence of events

conflict : a clash or struggle between people, ideas, or feelings; characters can have a conflict within themselves, with another character, with society, or with nature

protagonist (proh-TAG-uh-nist) : the main character; the character around whom the action of the plot centers

resolution : the solution or working out of a literary conflict

subplot : a story line or plot that is secondary to the main plot

theme : the main message that an author wants to communicate to a reader

LEARN
Activity 1: *Twelfth Night* - Act V *(Online)*

Activity 2: *Twelfth Night* - Act V *(Offline)*
Instructions
Vocabulary for Act V:

dissembling: lying

durance: being held by force

semblance: outward appearance

notorious: well-known in an unfavorable way

recompense: something given in return

estate: one's social rank and physical inheritance

Activity 3: *Twelfth Night* - Act V *(Online)*

Activity 4: Happy Endings *(Online)*

Activity 5: Thoughts and Themes *(Offline)*
Instructions
The themes in Shakespeare's famous plays have contributed to the way people today understand big questions about love and war, life and death, and what is the right way to act and live. Compare your own ideas to the themes you find in *Twelfth Night* as you answer the questions below.

1. In Act II, when Malvolio says, "All is fortune," he means that everything that happens to a character is based on circumstances that are out of the character's control. To what extent is Malvolio correct? In *Twelfth Night*, do the characters' fates depend more on outside circumstances or on their own traits and choices? Give examples from the text to support your answer.

    _____
    _____
    _____
    _____

2. Fools and foolishness are important themes in *Twelfth Night*. Describe the difference between the two kinds of fools the reader meets in the play.

    _____
    _____
    _____
    _____
    _____

3. What does Shakespeare say about love in *Twelfth Night*? Do you agree or disagree? Support your ideas with evidence from the text.

    _____
    _____
    _____
    _____
    _____

Student Guide
Lesson 7: Reflection, or What You Will

Boogie with the Bard! Find out how Shakespeare used music in his plays. Also, review what you have learned in this unit and see if you can unlock the 400-year-old mystery behind the title of *Twelfth Night*.

Lesson Objectives

- Demonstrate knowledge of authors, characters, and events of historically or culturally significant works of literature.
- Describe characters based on speech, actions, or interactions with others.
- Identify character traits and motivations.
- Identify defining characteristics of drama.
- Identify theme.

PREPARE

Approximate lesson time is 60 minutes.

Materials

For the Student

📖 Selections from Twelfth Night: Act 2, Scene 4

Classics for Young Readers, Vol. 6: An Audio Companion - Track 29

Keywords and Pronunciation

plot : what happens in a story; the sequence of events

foreshadowing : a technique authors use to give clues about or to suggest what is going to happen

mood : the emotions or feelings conveyed in a literary work

subplot : a story line or plot that is secondary to the main plot

theme : the main message that an author wants to communicate to a reader

---

LEARN
Activity 1: Reflection, or *What You Will* (Online)

Activity 2: *Twelfth Night* (Offline)

Activity 3: The Power of Song (Online)

Activity 4: *Twelfth Night*, or *What you Will* (Offline)
Instructions

Reread the song Feste sings to close the play:

When that I was and a little tiny boy,
With hey, ho, the wind and the rain,
A foolish thing was but a toy,
For the rain it raineth every day.

But when I came to man's estate
With hey, ho, the wind and the rain,
'Gainst knaves and thieves men shut their gate,
For the rain it raineth every day.

But when I came, alas! To wive,
With hey, ho, the wind and the rain,
By swaggering could I never thrive
For the rain it raineth every day.

A great while ago the world begun,
With hey, ho, the wind and the rain,
But that's all one, our play is done,
And we'll strive to please you every day!
For the rain it raineth every day

With what message does Shakespeare end *Twelfth Night*? Does Feste encourage the audience not to be foolish, not to take things too seriously, or are both messages part of the **theme?** Support your analysis with a evidence from the text.

_____

_____

_____

_____

In the last lines of the last song in *Twelfth Night,* you see how a phrase can have a double meaning or refer to two different things at the same time. Much to the delight of audiences and readers, Shakespeare's plays and poetry are full of double meanings. So it might happen that as a person watches a play like *Twelfth Night*, even if he has seen it 10 times before, he might suddenly hear or understand something new.

But Twelfth Night is especially exceptional among Shakespeare's plays because it is his only text that bears two titles. Originally, the play was titled *Twelfth Night*, or *What You Will*. And if Shakespeare ever explained why he did it, like so much of the information about him, it has been lost.

People today still wonder why the play has two titles. Some people think Shakespeare titled it *What You Will*, which could be read as, "Call It Whatever You Want to," to reflect all of the confusion in the play and the notion that anything could happen. Others think he titled it *What You Will* to show that even though the characters endured good and bad luck, they could always choose how they acted, and that their choices, more than fate, affected how their stories ended.

Think about the events of the play, then decide: Why do you think Shakespeare titled the play *Twelfth Night*, or *What You Will*? Give evidence to support your analysis.

_____

_____

_____

_____

Activity 5. Optional: Reflection, or *What You Will* (Online)

Name

Date

Selections from *Twelfth Night*
Track 32, Act 2, Scene 4

DUKE ORSINO:
Give me some music. Now, good morrow, friends.
Now, good Cesario, but that piece of song,
That old and antique song we heard last night:
Methought it did relieve my passion much,
More than **light airs** and **recollected** terms
Of these most brisk and giddy-paced times:
Come, but one verse.

CURIO:
He is not here, so please your lordship that should sing it.

DUKE ORSINO:
Who was it?

CURIO:
Feste, the jester, my lord; a fool that the lady
Olivia's father took much delight in. He is about the
house.

DUKE ORSINO:
Seek him out, and play the tune the while.

[Exit CURIO. Music plays]

Come hither, boy: if ever thou shalt love,
In the sweet pangs of it remember me;
For such as I am all true lovers are,
Unstaid and **skittish** in all motions else,
Save in the constant image of the creature
That is beloved. How dost thou like this tune?

VIOLA:
It gives a very echo to the seat
Where Love is throned.

DUKE ORSINO:
Thou dost speak **masterly**:
My life upon't, young though thou art, thine eye
Hath stay'd upon some favour that it loves:
Hath it not, boy?

VIOLA:
A little, by your favor.

DUKE ORSINO:
What kind of woman is't?

VIOLA:
Of your **complexion**.

DUKE ORSINO:
Play music for me. Good-day, my friends. Come here,
Cesario. Let us listen to that song from olden times we
heard last night. It soothed me more than the light-
hearted songs and passing ditties of these fast and
crazy times. Sing just one verse.

CURIO:
The man whose singing pleased you is not here.

DUKE ORSINO:
Who was the singer?

CURIO:
Feste, a jester whom Olivia's father very much
enjoyed. He is in the house.

DUKE ORSINO:
Find him and bring him here. Until then, play the tune.

[Exit CURIO. Music plays]

Come here, boy. If you ever fall in love, when you are
truly feeling it, remember me. I am what all true lovers
are: undisciplined and restless in all things except in
thinking about my beloved, whose image is always in
my mind. Do you like this music?

VIOLA:
It echoes in the place where love sits (in my heart).

DUKE ORSINO:
You speak very well. My word, even though you are
young, your eyes have found someone you find
favorable, and you have fallen in love. Haven't you?

VIOLA:
A little, if you approve.

DUKE ORSINO:
What does she look like?

VIOLA:
Of your looks. (She looks like you.)

Name   Date

DUKE ORSINO:
She is not worth thee, then. What years, i' faith?

VIOLA:
About your years, my lord.

DUKE ORSINO:
Too old by heaven: let still the woman take
An elder than herself: so wears she to him,
So sways she level in her husband's heart:
For, boy, however we do praise ourselves,
Our fancies are more **giddy** and unfirm,
More longing, wavering, sooner lost and worn,
Than women's are.

VIOLA:
I think it well, my lord.

DUKE ORSINO:
Then let thy love be younger than thyself,
Or thy affection cannot hold the bent;
For women are as roses, whose fair flower
Being once display'd, doth fall that very hour.

VIOLA:
And so they are: alas, that they are so;
To die, even when they to perfection grow!

[Re-enter CURIO and Clown]

DUKE ORSINO:
O, fellow, come, the song we had last night.
Mark it, Cesario, it is old and plain;
The **spinsters** and the knitters in the sun
And the free maids that weave their thread with bones
Do use to chant it: it is silly **sooth,**
And **dallies** with the innocence of love,
Like the old age.

Clown: Are you ready, sir?

DUKE ORSINO: Ay; prithee, sing.

[Music]

SONG.
Clown:
Come away, come away, death,
And in sad cypress let me be laid;
Fly away, fly away breath;
I am slain by a fair cruel maid.
My shroud of white, stuck all with **yew,**
O, prepare it!
My part of death, no one so true, so true
Did share it.

DUKE ORSINO:
Then she is not good enough for you. How old is she?

VIOLA:
She is about as old as you are, my lord.

DUKE ORSINO: She is too old! A woman should marry a man that is older than she is so that she always has her husband's heart. No matter how much we value our love, our fancies come and go much more quickly than women's do.

VIOLA:
I think that's a good idea, my lord.

DUKE ORSINO:
Then your love should be younger than you are, or else it will not last. Because women are like roses: the moment they bloom, they begin to fade.

VIOLA:
That is true. How sad it is that when they are perfect, they must begin to wither and die.

[Re-enter Curio and Clown]

DUKE ORSINO:
Sing us the song you sang last night. Notice, Cesario, it is old and plain. The old women who never married and the young maids who are not yet married sing it. It is silly and does not take the innocence of love seriously.

Clown: Are you ready, sir?

DUKE ORSINO: Yes, please sing.

[Music]

SONG
Clown:
Come away, come away, death,
And in sad cypress let me be laid;
Fly away, fly away breath;
I am slain by a fair cruel maid.
My shroud of white, stuck all with yew,
O, prepare it!
My part of death, no one so true, so true
Did share it.

Name _____   Date _____

Not a flower, not a flower sweet
On my black coffin let there be strown;
Not a friend, not a friend greet

My poor corpse, where my bones shall be thrown:
A thousand thousand sighs to save,
Lay me, O, where
Sad true lover never find my grave,
To weep there!

DUKE ORSINO: There's for thy pains.

Clown: No pains, sir: I take pleasure in singing, sir.

DUKE ORSINO: I'll pay thy pleasure then.

Clown: Truly, sir, and pleasure will be paid, one time or another.

DUKE ORSINO: Give me now leave to leave thee.

Clown:
Now, the **melancholy** god protect thee; and the tailor make thy **doublet** of changeable **taffeta**, for thy mind is a very **opal**. I would have men of such constancy put to sea, that their business might be every thing and their intent every where; for that's it that always makes a good voyage of nothing. Farewell.

[Exit]

DUKE ORSINO: Let all the rest give place.

[CURIO and Attendants retire]

DUKE ORSINO: Once more, Cesario,
Get thee to yond same sovereign cruelty:
Tell her, my love, more noble than the world,
Prizes not quantity of dirty lands;
The parts that fortune hath **bestow'd** upon her,
Tell her, I hold as giddily as fortune;
But 'tis that miracle and queen of gems
That nature **pranks** her in attracts my soul.

VIOLA: But if she cannot love you, sir?

DUKE ORSINO: I cannot be so answer'd.

Not a flower, not a flower sweet
On my black coffin let there be strown;
Not a friend, not a friend greet

My poor corpse, where my bones shall be thrown:
A thousand thousand sighs to save,
Lay me, O, where
Sad true lover never find my grave,
To weep there!

DUKE ORSINO: Here is money for the trouble you took to sing your song.

Clown: It is no trouble to sing, sir; I enjoy it.

DUKE ORSINO: So I'll pay you for having enjoyed yourself.

Clown: We will all pay for enjoying ourselves eventually.

DUKE ORSINO: Allow me to bid you farewell.

Clown: May the god of your melancholy protect you, and may the tailor make you a short jacket of shiny, multi-colored women's skirts, because you are so fickle, and your thoughts so scattered that they are like a jewel that reflects many different colors. I would send men like you to sea, so that they might concern themselves with everything and plan to go everywhere, because that's the only way to accomplish some good from such wandering thoughts.

[Exit]

DUKE ORSINO: It is time for everyone to leave.

[Curio and Attendants retire]

DUKE ORSINO: Cesario, go back to Olivia and tell her that my love is so noble that I do not care about her lands or her wealth or anything else fortune has given her. I am attracted to her beauty and her spirit.

VIOLA: What if she cannot love you, sir?

DUKE ORSINO: I cannot accept that answer.

Name _____ **Date** _____

VIOLA: Sooth, but you must. Say that some lady, as perhaps there is, Hath for your love as a great a pang of heart As you have for Olivia: you cannot love her; You tell her so; must she not then be answer'd?	VIOLA: True, but you must. What if there were a lady, and maybe there is, who loves you as much as you love Olivia. But if you cannot love her, and tell her so, must she not accept that answer?
DUKE ORSINO: There is no woman's sides Can bide the beating of so strong a passion As love doth give my heart; no woman's heart So big, to hold so much; Their love may be call'd appetite, No motion of the liver, but the palate, That suffer **surfeit**, **cloyment** and revolt; But mine is all as hungry as the sea, And can digest as much: make no compare Between that love a woman can bear me And that I owe Olivia.	DUKE ORSINO: No woman could hold as strong a love as mine. No woman's heart is as big or could hold as much passion as mine. A woman's love might be called an appetite--not love from deep inside, but a passing sweetness that she could have too much of, grow sick of, or reject entirely. My love has no bounds and covers all things. Do not compare the love a woman could have for me and that I have pledged to Olivia.
VIOLA: Ay, but I know--	VIOLA: Yes, but I know--
DUKE ORSINO: What dost thou know?	DUKE ORSINO: What do you know?
VIOLA: Too well what love women to men may owe: In faith, they are as true of heart as we. My father had a daughter loved a man, As it might be, perhaps, were I a woman, I should your lordship.	VIOLA: I know how strongly a woman might love a man. They are as true of heart as we are. My father had a daughter who loved a man, as, if I were a woman, I would love you.
DUKE ORSINO: And what's her history?	DUKE ORSINO: And what happened to her?
VIOLA: A blank, my lord. She never told her love, But let concealment, like a worm i' the bud, Feed on her damask cheek: she pined in thought, And with a green and yellow melancholy She sat like Patience on a monument, Smiling at grief. Was not this love indeed? We men may say more, swear more: but indeed Our shows are more than will; for still we prove Much in our vows, but little in our love.	VIOLA: Her history is blank. She never told the man that she loved him. Instead, she hid her love, and it ate away at her like a worm in a flower. She was wistful, sickly, and sad, but sat like a statue of Patience, smiling at her grief. Was this not love indeed? We men may say more and swear more, but even though we promise much, we do little in our love.
DUKE ORSINO: But died thy sister of her love, my boy?	DUKE ORSINO: But did your sister die of her love, Cesario?
VIOLA: I am all the daughters of my father's house, And all the brothers too: and yet I know not. Sir, shall I to this lady?	VIOLA: I am all the daughters of my father's house, and all the brothers, too: and yet I do not know. Sir, shall I go to Olivia's house?
DUKE ORSINO: Ay, that's the theme. To her in haste; give her this jewel; say, My love can give no place, bide no **denay.**	DUKE ORSINO: Yes, that's the idea. Hurry there and give her this jewel. Tell her my love cannot be refused or rejected.
[Exit]	[Exit]

Name_____ Date_____

Vocabulary:

light airs: simple, pleasant songs
recollected: remembered
unstaid: lacking self-restraint
skittish: fidgety; refusing to be controlled
masterly: with exceptional skill
complexion: one's face and skin
giddy: likely to change or spin around
spinsters: women who have never married
sooth: true
dallies: to play with something without taking it seriously
melancholy: sad and thoughtful
yew: pieces of woods from the yew tree, which was often planted in cemeteries to symbolize grief
doublet: a jacket
taffeta: a shiny fabric used to make women's clothing
opal: a gem that reflects many colors
bestowed: given as a gift
pranks: to dress someone
sides: the outer measure of a thing
surfeit: disgust caused by excess
cloyment: to become sick of something pleasing from having too much
denay: denial

Student Guide
Lesson 8: Unit Assessment

Lesson Objectives

- Demonstrate knowledge of authors, characters, and events of historically or culturally significant works of literature.
- Describe characters based on speech, actions, or interactions with others.
- Identify and interpret the use of subplots.
- Identify character traits and motivations.
- Identify conflict and resolution.
- Identify defining characteristics of drama.
- Identify theme.
- Recognize the effect of setting or culture on a literary work.
- Recognize use of language to convey mood.

PREPARE

Approximate lesson time is 60 minutes.

ASSESS

Unit Assessment: *Twelfth Night* (*Online*)

Print the Unit Assessment page before you answer the online questions. When you finish these questions, read the Unit Assessment page and write your answers in your Reading Notebook.

Student Guide
Lesson 1: "Moses: The Long Journey Through the Wilderness"

Could you be a leader in a time of crisis? What if that crisis lasted for 40 years? Meet one man who brought his people out of slavery and led them until they reached their homeland--40 years later.

Lesson Objectives

- Demonstrate knowledge of authors, characters, and events of historically or culturally significant works of literature.
- Describe characters based on speech, action, or interactions with others.
- Identify character traits and motivations.
- Analyze connections between literature and life.
- Contribute meaningfully to group discussions by being prepared for discussion, drawing on preparation, explaining own ideas, building upon others' comments, and asking questions.

PREPARE

Approximate lesson time is 60 minutes.

Advance Preparation

- In the next unit, students will have the opportunity to select a novel to read and then complete the associated lessons. Review the list of novels and obtain a copy of the desired book. Some novels contain content that may be sensitive for some users. Please check the Course Introduction for more information.

Materials

For the Student

MLA Handbook for Writers of Research Papers - MLA (Modern Language Association) Full citation: MLA Handbook for Writers of Research Papers. 7th ed. New York: MLA, 2009. Print.

Reading Notebook

Classics for Young Readers, Vol. 6 - pages 248-255

Optional

🖥 Guidelines for Peer Discussion

Keywords and Pronunciation

Exodus (EK-suh-duhs) : the Israelites´ long journey out of Egypt

---

LEARN
Activity 1: "Moses: The Long Journey Through the Wilderness" *(Online)*

Activity 2: "Moses: The Long Journey Through the Wilderness" *(Online)*

Activity 3: "Moses: The Long Journey Through the Wilderness" *(Online)*

Activity 4: "Moses: The Long Journey Through the Wilderness" *(Online)*

Activity 5: On Leadership *(Offline)*
Instructions
Consider the character traits that Moses and the Israelites display.

1. One reason Moses is successful as a leader is because he perseveres. Define perseverance in your own words.

   _____
   _____
   _____
   _____

2. Why do you think people who persevere often become leaders?

   _____
   _____
   _____
   _____

Activity 6. Optional: "Moses: The Long Journey Through the Wilderness" *(Online)*

Activity 7: Peer Discussion *(Offline)*

Guidelines for Peer Discussion

Share your thoughts, ideas, questions, and feelings about a text with a peer or others. Listen carefully to what everyone has to say about the text. During your discussion, follow these guidelines.

1. Be prepared to discuss your ideas about the text and to ask and answer questions about what you read. Whenever possible, use examples from the text to support your statements, help others understand your meaning, and justify your answers.

2. Listen carefully and quietly if it's not your turn to speak. Pay attention to what others say so that you can add your ideas. Speak clearly and in complete sentences.

3. Connect and add to the ideas that others have stated using sentences that begin with phrases such as:

   "I understand . . . ."
   "I feel that . . . ."
   "We should also think about how . . . ."
   "That idea relates to . . . ."

4. Respectfully question the opinions of others and politely defend your reasoning if your opinion differs. Use sentences that begin with phrases such as:

   "What do you mean when you say . . .?"
   "Can you give an example of . . .?"
   "I see what you're saying, but what about . . .?"
   "I reacted to that a little differently because . . . ."
   "I disagree with that because . . . ."

5. Draw conclusions about what has already happened in a text and make inferences about what may happen next.

6. Keep the goal(s) of the discussion in mind and respect others. Remember that each member of the group has a valuable contribution to make.

7. Remember that opinions are neither right nor wrong, only different. Remain cordial, thoughtful, and courteous when disagreements or differences of opinion occur.

Student Guide
Lesson 2: "The Fiery Furnace"

What happens when people's beliefs conflict with the law of the land? Step into the kingdom of Babylon in the 7th century B.C. and meet its powerful king and the three Israelites who dared to defy him.

Lesson Objectives

- Analyze connections between literature and life.
- Demonstrate knowledge of authors, characters, and events of historically or culturally significant works of literature.
- Describe characters based on speech, action, or interactions with others.
- Identify character traits and motivations.
- Identify conflict and resolution.

PREPARE

Approximate lesson time is 60 minutes.

Materials

For the Student

Classics for Young Readers, Vol. 6 - pages 256-259

Keywords and Pronunciation

abednego (uh-BED-nih-goh)

conflict : a clash or struggle between people, ideas, or feelings; characters can have a conflict within themselves, with another character, with society, or with nature

Nebuchadnezzar (neb-yuh-kud-NEH-zur)

LEARN
Activity 1: "The Fiery Furnace" *(Online)*

Activity 2: "The Fiery Furnace" *(Online)*

Activity 3: "The Fiery Furnace" *(Online)*

Activity 4: "The Fiery Furnace" *(Online)*

Activity 5: On Leadership *(Offline)*

Instructions

Answer these questions about courage based on your reading of "The Fiery Furnace."

1. Define courage in your own words.

_____

_____

_____

_____

2. Shadrach, Meshach, and Abednego were leaders in Babylon, and they are still remembered for their great courage. Why do you think courageous people often become leaders?

_____

_____

_____

_____

Activity 6. Optional: "The Fiery Furnace" *(Online)*

Student Guide
Lesson 3: "The Good Samaritan"

In this story, a man decides whether helping someone is an obligation or an opportunity.

Lesson Objectives

- Demonstrate knowledge of authors, characters, and events of historically or culturally significant works of literature.
- Describe characters based on speech, action, or interactions with others.
- Identify character traits and motivations.
- Analyze connections between literature and life.
- Recognize author's purpose and devices used to accomplish it, including author's language, organization, and structure.

PREPARE

Approximate lesson time is 60 minutes.

Materials

For the Student

Classics for Young Readers, Vol. 6 - page 260

Keywords and Pronunciation

parable : a story that illustrates a principle or teaching

LEARN
Activity 1: "The Good Samaritan" *(Online)*

Activity 2: "The Good Samaritan" *(Online)*

Activity 3: "The Good Samaritan" *(Online)*

Activity 4: "The Good Samaritan" *(Online)*

Activity 5: Leadership *(Offline)*

Instructions

You have read the parable of "The Good Samaritan" and considered what it means to "love they neighbor as thyself." Now answer some final questions about compassion.

1. Define *compassion* in your own words.

   _____

   _____

   _____

   _____

   _____

   _____

   _____

   _____

2. Jesus uses the story of the Samaritan as an example of the right way to treat people. Why do you think people who show compassion without prejudice are often an example and inspiration to others?

   _____

   _____

   _____

   _____

   _____

   _____

   _____

   _____

Activity 6. Optional: "The Good Samaritan" *(Online)*

Student Guide
Lesson 4: Reflection

Lesson Objectives

- Compare and contrast literary characters and selections.
- Demonstrate knowledge of authors, characters, and events of historically or culturally significant works of literature.
- Describe characters based on speech, action, or interactions with others.
- Identify character traits and motivations.
- Analyze connections between literature and life.

PREPARE

Approximate lesson time is 60 minutes.

Advance Preparation

- In two weeks, for the Semester Review and Assessment unit, students will perform a formal recitation of a poem, and you will evaluate their performance. Students should have selected a poem during unit 12 of this semester, and they should have been practicing their recitation. You may wish to remind students that they will need to perform this piece in two weeks and encourage them to continue practicing and polishing their recitation.

Materials

For the Student

Optional

Classics for Young Readers, Vol. 6 - pages 248-260

Reading Notebook

LEARN
Activity 1: What a Character! *(Online)*

Activity 2: Reflection *(Online)*

Activity 3: On Leadership *(Online)*

Student Guide
Lesson 5: Unit Assessment

Lesson Objectives

- Analyze connections between literature and life.
- Compare and contrast literary characters and selections.
- Demonstrate knowledge of authors, characters, and events of historically or culturally significant works of literature.
- Describe characters based on speech, action, or interactions with others.
- Identify character traits and motivations.

PREPARE

Approximate lesson time is 60 minutes.

ASSESS

Unit Assessment: Stories from the Bible (*Online*)

Print the Assessment page before you answer the online questions. When you finish these questions, read the Assessment page and write your answers in your Reading Notebook.

Student Guide
Lesson 1: Recitation

Lesson Objectives

- Revise, proofread, and publish an essay.
- Evaluate strategies used by speakers in oral presentations.
- Make oral presentations.
- Use appropriate verbal and nonverbal techniques for oral presentations.
- Use strategies to enhance listening comprehension.

PREPARE

Approximate lesson time is 60 minutes.

Materials

For the Student

MLA Handbook for Writers of Research Papers - MLA (Modern Language Association) Full citation:

MLA Handbook for Writers of Research Papers. 7th ed. New York: MLA, 2009. Print.

Optional

📖 Preparing Poetry for Performance

Classics for Young Readers, Vol. 6

Classics for Young Readers, Vol. 6: An Audio Companion

Keywords and Pronunciation

alliteration : the use of words with the same or similar beginning sounds

allusion : a reference to a familiar literary or historical person or event, used to make an idea more easily understood

assonance : the repetition of similar vowel sounds in several words

figurative language : language that uses figures of speech such as metaphor, simile, and personification for poetic effect rather than for precise, factual meaning; for example, "Her eyes are like stars" is figurative language, in contrast to the literal use of "stars" in "The stars are shining tonight"

first-person point of view : narration of a story by one of the characters, using the first-person pronouns *I* and *me*

imagery : language that creates a mental picture by appealing to the senses, that makes readers see, hear, smell, taste, or feel things in their imagination; for example, "the coal-black night," "the stinging cold," "the rapping and tapping of rain on the roof"

metaphor : a figure of speech that suggests or states a comparison between two unlike things, without using such words as *like* or *as*; for example, "The cat's eyes were emeralds shining in the night."

meter : the arrangement of words in poetry based on rhythm, accents, and the number of syllables in a line

mood : the emotions or feelings conveyed in a literary work

narrative poem : a poem that tells a story

onomatopoeia (AH-nuh-MAH-tuh-PEE-uh) : the use of words that imitate sounds, such as buzz, clang, boom

rhyme scheme : the pattern of rhymes made by the final words or sounds in the lines of a poem, typically designated by a different letter of the alphabet to represent each rhyme

rhyming couplet : two consecutive lines of poetry that rhyme

rhythm : a regular pattern of sound and beats within a poem

theme : the main message that an author wants to communicate to a reader

tone : the writer's attitude toward the topic or subject

LEARN
Activity 1: Recite Your Poem *(Offline)*

ASSESS
Lesson Checkpoint: Recitation (*Offline*)

It's time to check what you have learned.

1. Gather the Assessment Sheet.
2. Read and follow the instructions to complete the Presentation.
3. When you've finished, your Learning Coach will review your work and enter the results online.

LEARN
Activity 2. Optional: Recitation *(Online)*

Preparing Poetry for Performance

Many of the world's greatest writers, such as Homer, Basho, and Shakespeare, express their ideas through poetry. Soon, you will have the opportunity to share with an audience a famous poem that you enjoy or that is meaningful to you. Use these tips, pointers, and questions to prepare your poem for performance.

A. Express Yourself

Perhaps you chose your poem because you like the subject, agree with the theme, or admire its images or the way it sounds. You can communicate your and the poet's feelings to your audience using expressive speaking techniques.

First, decide what feeling or idea you want to communicate to your audience. For example, in a poem about a faithful dog, you might want to emphasize that dogs are brave and loyal companions. In a poem about friendship, you might want your audience to think about what it means to be a good friend. In a nonsense poem, you might want your audience to enjoy the sounds or humorous images.

Next, explore how you can use your voice to influence the way your audience experiences the poem. You might want to emphasize certain words to create the poem's mood or use a particular tone of voice, perhaps a fearful, surprised, joyful, or tender tone, to convey the speaker's feelings.

Then, find any "special effects" the poet included in his or her poem, such as assonance, alliteration, or an unusual rhythm. Decide how you want to use your voice to draw your audience's attention to these features. For example, you might add a pause or make a particular effort to preserve the poet's meter.

If you wish, make notes on a copy of your poem to remind you where to put emphasis, breaths, pauses, and gestures to create the mood you want.

B. Tongue Untied

To make the greatest impact on their audiences, performers speak clearly as well as expressively. The best speakers *enunciate,* or correctly and clearly pronounce, each word.

Practice your enunciation skills with these tongue twisters. To recite a tongue twister correctly, begin by saying it slowly and clearly pronouncing each syllable of each word. As you become more comfortable with it, try to say it correctly at normal speed *and* with expression. For example, once you become comfortable reciting the phrase, "Sally sells seashells by the seashore," you might try to say it as if you are surprised that she is there.

1. Sally sells seashells by the seashore.
2. A box of biscuits, a box of mixed biscuits, and a biscuit-mixer.
3. Red leather, yellow leather; red letter, yellow letter.

When you finish, practice reciting your poem clearly *and* expressively. You might want to practice by recording your recitation on tape so you can adjust your performance as necessary.

C. Standing Tall
A performer's body is as powerful an instrument as his or her voice. You can use facial expressions, such as a smile, a frown, or a puzzled look, to help you communicate what is happening in the poem. You may also use gestures, such as waving your hand, shrugging your shoulders, or nodding your head, where appropriate.

Once you decide which, if any, facial expressions and gestures you want to use, practice them while looking in a mirror until you become comfortable speaking and moving at the same time.

Finally, to engage your audience's attention, be sure to:
- Stand straight and tall.
- Speak clearly and loud enough so that everyone can hear you.
- Make eye contact with the audience when reciting. If you are reading from a book or paper, hold it low enough for the audience to see your face. While reading aloud, occasionally pause and look up.

D. Get Ready, Get Set, Recite!
You've decided how you want to present your poem and practiced your skills. Now take a deep breath, relax, and have fun: it's time to recite your poem!

Student Guide
Lesson 2: Semester Review

Lesson Objectives

- Compare and contrast literary characters and selections.
- Demonstrate comprehension of text.
- Demonstrate knowledge of authors, characters, and events of historically or culturally significant works of literature.
- Describe characters by speech, actions, or interactions with others.
- Identify alliteration.
- Identify and interpret the use of figurative language.
- Identify and interpret the use of subplots.
- Identify character traits and motivations.
- Identify characteristics of haiku.
- Identify conflict and resolution.
- Identify defining characteristics of the text.
- Identify irony.
- Identify personification.
- Identify speaker.
- Identify theme.
- Make inferences and draw conclusions.
- Recognize author's attitude or tone.
- Recognize author's purpose and devices used to accomplish it, including author's language, organization, and structure.
- Recognize the effect of setting or culture on a literary work.
- Recognize use of language to convey mood.

PREPARE

Approximate lesson time is 60 minutes.

LEARN
Activity 1: Intermediate Literature A (Online)

Student Guide
Lesson 3: Semester Assessment

Lesson Objectives

- Compare and contrast literary characters and selections.
- Demonstrate knowledge of authors, characters, and events of historically or culturally significant works of literature.
- Describe characters by speech, actions, or interactions with others.
- Identify alliteration.
- Identify and interpret the use of figurative language.
- Identify character traits and motivations.
- Identify characteristics of haiku.
- Identify conflict and resolution.
- Identify defining characteristics of the text.
- Identify irony.
- Identify speaker.
- Identify theme.
- Make inferences and draw conclusions.
- Recognize author's attitude or tone.
- Recognize author's purpose and devices used to accomplish it, including author's language, organization, and structure.
- Recognize use of language to convey mood.
- Use an effective pattern of organization.
- Use complete sentences and correct capitalization, punctuation, and spelling.
- Write an essay that contains an introduction, thesis statement, supporting paragraphs, and conclusion.

PREPARE

Approximate lesson time is 60 minutes.

ASSESS

Semester Assessment: Intermediate Literature A - Grade 6 (*Online*)

Print the Assessment page and the Readings page before you answer the online questions. You will need the Readings page to answer some of the online questions. When you finish these questions, read the Assessment page and write your answers in your Reading Notebook.

Name   Date

Semester Assessment

Readings

Answer questions online about the three readings presented here.

Alexander and the Gordian Knot
adapted from "The Gordian Knot" by James Baldwin

Once there was a king of Phrygia named Gordius who bound an ox yoke to a wagon's pole with a rope. He fastened it so deftly that the ends of the rope were hidden and no one could see how to undo it.

In time, it came to be believed that the person who could undo the wonderful knot would have the world for his kingdom. Every year, a great many men came to see the Gordian knot. Princes and warriors from every land tried to untie it, but the ends of the rope remained hidden, and they could not even make a beginning of the task.

Hundreds of years had passed when there came into Phrygia a young king from Macedonia, a country far across the sea. The young king's name was Alexander. He had conquered all Greece, crossed over into Asia with a small army of chosen men, and had beaten the king of Persia in a battle.

"Where is the Gordian knot?" he asked.

The Phrygians led him to the temple where the little wagon stood with the yoke and wagon pole, just as Gordius had left it.

"What was it that is said about this knot?" Alexander asked.

"It is said that the man who undoes the knot shall have the world for his kingdom."

Alexander looked at the knot carefully. He could not find the ends of the rope, but what did that matter? He raised his sword and, with one stroke, cut it into so many pieces that the yoke fell to the ground.

"It is thus," said the young king, "that I cut all Gordian knots."

Then he went on with his little army to conquer Asia.

"The world is my kingdom," he said.

_____

yoke: a bar or frame for harnessing animals to pull an object, such as a wagon or a plow
deftly: skillfully

Name   Date

The Spartans Speak
adapted from "A Laconic Answer" by James Baldwin

In ancient Greece, some of the people in the southern part of the country were called Spartans, and they were noted for their simple habits and their bravery. The name of their land was Laconia, and so they were sometimes called Lacons.

One of the unusual rules that the Spartans kept was that they should speak briefly and never use more words than were needed. They came to be known for their brief sayings, which said much with few words. Today, a short answer is often spoken of as being *laconic;* that is, as being such an answer as a Lacon would be likely to give.

North of the Lacons, there was a land called Macedon, and this land was at one time ruled over by a warlike king named Philip. Philip of Macedon wanted to become the master of all Greece. So he raised a great army and made war upon the other states, until nearly all of them were forced to call him their king. Then he sent a letter to the Spartans in Laconia and said, "If I go down into your country, I will level your great city to the ground."

In a few days, an answer was brought back to him. When he opened the letter, he found only one word written there.

That word was *if.*

Name   Date

Semester Assessment

Untitled
by Basho

Spring morning marvel
lovely nameless little hill
on a sea of mist

———————————

marvel: wonder

April
by Sara Teadsdale

The roofs are shining from the rain,
The sparrows twitter as they fly
And with a windy April grace
The little clouds go by.

Yet the backyards are bare and brown
With only one unchanging tree –
I could not be sure of Spring,
Save that it sings in me.

———————————

save: except